Ready, Booted, and Spurred

Ready, Booted, and Spurred

Arkansas in the U.S.-Mexican War

William A. Frazier &
Mark K. Christ, Editors

Contributors:

Donald S. Frazier

C. Fred Williams

William A. Frazier

Pedro Santoni

Elliott West

BUTLER CENTER BOOKS

Little Rock, Arkansas

BUTLER
CENTER

BOOKS

The Butler Center for Arkansas Studies
Central Arkansas Library System
100 Rock Street
Little Rock, Arkansas 72201

First Edition, 2009

ISBN (hardback) 978-1-935106-05-0
10-digit ISBN (hardback) 1-935106-05-8
Hardback printing: 10 9 8 7 6 5 4 3 2 1

ISBN (paperback) 978-0-9800897-5-2
10-digit ISBN (paperback) 0-9800897-5-1
Paperback printing: 10 9 8 7 6 5 4 3 2 1

Acquired for Butler Center Books by David Stricklin
Project manager: Ted Parkhurst
Book design and cover design: H. K. Stewart
Proofreader: Rod Lorenzen

The editors secured the photographs and illustrations used in this book.

Library of Congress Catalog Card Number: 2008939483

Printed in the United States of America

This book is printed on archival-quality paper that meets requirements
of the American National Standard for Information Sciences,
Permanence of Paper, Printed Library Materials, ANSI Z39.48-1984.

Table of Contents

Contributors

Mark K. Christ is community outreach director for the Arkansas Historic Preservation Program. He joined the AHPP in 1990 after working as a professional journalist. A 1982 graduate of the University of Arkansas at Little Rock, he received his Master's degree in 2000 from the University of Oklahoma. He has coordinated the Old State House Museum's series of annual history seminars since 2002. He has edited several books, including *"Rugged and Sublime" The Civil War in Arkansas, Sentinels of History: Reflections on Arkansas Properties Listed on the National Register of Historic Places*, which won an Award of Merit from the American Association for State and Local History, *"Getting Used To Being Shot At": The Spence Family Civil War Letters, "All Cut to Pieces and Gone to Hell": The Civil War, Race Relations and the Battle of Poison Spring*, and *"The Earth Shook and Trees Trembled": Civil War Arkansas 1863-1864*. The University of Oklahoma Press will publish his next book, *"This is no Raid of the Enemy": The Struggle for the Arkansas River Valley*, in 2009.

Donald S. Frazier is a professor in the history department of McMurry University. He is the author of two books including *Blood and Treasure: Confederate Empire in the Southwest* (Texas A&M, 1995) and *Cottonclads! The Battle of Galveston and the Defense of the Texas Coast* (McWhiney Foundation Press, 1996). He is also the general editor of *The U.S. and Mexico at War: Nineteenth Century Expansionism and Conflict* published in 1998 by Macmillan Library Reference. When not teaching or serving on civic boards, Dr. Frazier is also President and CEO of the McWhiney Foundation, a non-profit organization dedicated to promoting history education. In that capacity he is involved in the management of a history publishing company, research center, and the Buffalo Gap Historic Village, an outdoor building museum near Abilene. For fun he is an enthusiastic heritage tourism consumer and can be found prowling battlefields from the Llano Estacado to the beaches of Normandy.

William A. Frazier has a BA and MA in history from the University of Memphis. His graduate work there focused on antebellum America and the U.S.-Mexican War. He is a journalist in Memphis and works for *The Commercial Appeal* newspaper. Before moving to Memphis, he was a writer and editor for the *Arkansas Democrat*. He is a native of Hot Springs, Arkansas.

Pedro Santoni, who holds degrees from the University of Notre Dame, the University of Puerto Rico, and El Colegio de México, is Professor of History and Department Chair at California State University, San Bernardino. He is the author of *Mexican at Arms: Puro Federalists and the Politics of War, 1845-1848* (Fort Worth: Texas Christian University Press, 1996), and of various articles on the political, military, and cultural history of nineteenth-century Mexico. Professor Santoni also served as associate editor of *The United States and Mexico at War: Nineteenth-Century Expansionism and Conflict* (New York: MacMillan Publishing Company, 1998), and is the editor of *Daily Lives of Civilians in Wartime Latin America: From the Wars of Independence to the Central American Civil Wars* (Westport, Conn.: Greenwood Press, 2008).

Elliott West, Alumni Distinguished Professor of History at the University of Arkansas, Fayetteville, is a specialist in the history of the American West. He is author of six books, more than 20 chapters in books and more than 50 articles. He has written on topics ranging from western saloons to frontier childhood and the environmental history of the Great Plains. *The Contested Plains* (1998) received the Caughey Prize as the year's outstanding work in western history and the Francis Parkman Prize as the best book in American history. He has twice won his university's award as the year's outstanding teacher.

C. Fred Williams is Professor of History at the University of Arkansas at Little Rock where he teaches courses on the American West and Arkansas History. He has authored and/or co-edited eight books including *Arkansas: Independent and Proud*, published by the American Historical Press in 2002, and *Historic Little Rock: An Illustrated History* (San Antonio: Historical Publishing Network, 2008).

Introduction

In the spring of 2002, the Old State House Museum set out to examine Arkansas's role in the U.S.-Mexican War. While it has gone largely unnoticed, it is a compelling, and often troubling, aspect of Arkansas and American history. Not only is the 1846-48 conflict the first large-scale military operation in which the state participated, it is arguably the first truly foreign war that the United States fought. Too, the end of the war offers an interesting marker in the state's history. Its 1848 Treaty of Guadalupe Hidalgo marked a twelve-year median between Arkansas becoming a state in 1836 and the election of 1860, which ultimately led to Arkansas severing its bonds with the United States in the Civil War.

In conjunction with the 2005-06 exhibit "Try Us: Arkansas in the U.S.-Mexican War," the Old State House Museum on Aug. 20, 2005, sponsored a one-day seminar titled "Ready, Booted and Spurred: Arkansas and the U.S.-Mexican War." The participants at the seminar heard five speakers discuss events leading up to the state's involvement, its military, its post-war years, the national impact of the conflict, and a glimpse of how Mexican historians of the period viewed the event. The essays in this publication are the result of that seminar.

C. Fred Williams, professor of history at the University of Arkansas at Little Rock, set the stage for Arkansas's involvement in the Mexican conflict with a look at the state's view of its frontier, an overarching concern for its early settlers. Bill Frazier, a guest curator of the "Try Us" exhibit, offered a survey of Arkansas's military during the war. Pedro Santoni, department of history chair at California State University, San Bernardino, explained how the early Mexican history of the war has held up to scrutiny by modern historians. Donald S. Frazier, professor of history at McMurry

University, delivered a strong example of the fluidity of Arkansan and American life during the antebellum period. Elliott West, distinguished professor of history at the University of Arkansas at Fayetteville, wove a broad view of the impact that the acquisition of territory from Mexico made on Arkansas and the United States.

As demographics in Arkansas and America change with the Mexican immigration of the early twenty-first century, a glimpse at a more turbulent time of two peoples may better help Arkansans of all backgrounds better understand their shared legacy of that war.

The seminar "Ready, Booted and Spurred: Arkansas and the U.S.-Mexican War," as well as the publication of the essays from it, was made possible by the Old State House Museum, an agency of the Department of Arkansas Heritage. Bill Gatewood, Georganne Sisco, Larry Ahart, Gail Moore, Joellen Maack, Ian Beard and Amy Peck of the Old State House staff were key partners in the seminar, as was Mark K. Christ of the Arkansas Historic Preservation Program. Donald S. Frazier and the McWhiney Foundation encouraged publication of the seminar proceedings from the project's early stages. Thanks to David Stricklin and the staff of the Butler Center for Arkansas Studies, Central Arkansas Library System, Little Rock, for all of their assistance and encouragement in publishing this volume. Pedro Santoni would like to thank Paul Vanderwood, who read an earlier version of his essay, for his comments and insights.

William A. Frazier and Mark K. Christ
February 7, 2006

From Murfreesboro to Buena Vista

By Donald S. Frazier

This gathering, this conference, I understand is usually a Civil War symposium. I had been tasked by my hosts to bridge the gap between that great conflict and the lesser understood but vastly important War with Mexico. I will begin this journey, then, by reading to you a letter from Matt Riddick, a native of Georgia but resident of Arkansas, to his friend Augustus Valerius Ball, a fellow Georgian but a more recent resident of Texas.[1]

Shelbyvill Tenn. Feb 11 1863

My Dear Friend Gus,

Yesterday evening your favor of December 24 was placed in my hands—the first line I have had from you in nearly five years and how glad I was to hear from you once more over your own name, I cannot attempt to tell. Five years, Gus, is a long time in our short lives, but how quick has the past five slided by—how very quick to me. It seemed but yesterday when you and I met the last time. Do you now remember where? At my father's house in Randolph County, and how we briefly but in perfect good faith and happy, promised ourselves a home in the west. It seems but yesterday I say—so vivid is the recollection of all to me. But that time is past and with it we should try to forget all sorrows and unpleasant memories yet these are thought I love to cherish, though painful they be. How best to fulfill my promise, Gus, I can't tell—for like you I have a thousand things to tell which my pen will fail to do. When I left home the 7th of Oct. 1858, it was with the settled determination mutually considered never to return to old Georgia again. When I left it was without the knowledge of any one save brother John in whose hands I placed my unsettled business. I did not know my self where I should go. I taken the train ... on the evening of the 8th and run up to Atlanta that night; here I changed all my paper money off for gold and silver and bought what few articles of clothing I needed. I took the cars at this place for Chattanooga at 9:00 the 9th in company with Dr. Walker. In answer to his questions I gave Chattanooga as my destination—but no sooner arrived here than I got on the night train for Nashville which place I reached about sunup on the 10th. William Chapman, John Blocker and seven others of my old school mates and acquaintances were here attending lectures in the Medical School. I spent that day (Sunday) with them in attending church and walking over the city. To their several inquiries, "where did you come from where are you going" I gave evasive answers and left earlier the following morning by stage for the Louisville RR depot. I reached Louisville, Kentucky without anything of special occurrence. Here I found a young man from Columbus, Georgia whose name I have forgotten and as we were both traveling the same way we soon formed an acquaintance. I spent but a few hours in Louisville but crossed the Ohio river at night and took the train at New Albany Indiana for Springfield Ill. But I changed my route a little and turned down to Cairo in the latter state. There we went ... aboard a fine steamer at night bound for Memphis which place we searched in safety without an incident. Here my traveling friend left me and I went on down to Napolean at the mouth of the Arkansas river without changing boats.

Here I formed an acquaintance of a very nice young man by the name of Jo Smith from Tullahoma, Tenn. As the Arkansas river was very low we had to go up White river on a very small but pleasant boat as far as Aberdeen and there take the stage for Little Rock—the railroad not being completed at that day. I arrived at Little Rock at night with about $100.00 in my pocket. I spent several days here in taking a breathing spell and looking around to see what was best to be done. I saw in the papers that Capt. Beal of the U.S. engineers was then in Fort Smith with a company of men equipped and on the point of leaving for the plains to survey an overland route to California. The idea pleased me and I took passage for Ft Smith.

But what was my surprise and chagrin to find on my arrival that I was one day too late—the party had left the day before. To this circumstance I am doubtless indebted for my present position in the [Confederate] *army, as I should probably have remained in California.*

I tarried but a few days in Ft. Smith when I went over to Van Burin and secured a situation as assistant teacher in a daily school at a fair salary. It was the first of Nov. when I entered on my duties and served in that capacity for two months when by mutual consent my employer and myself squared accounts. And on new years day 1859 I got aboard the "Violett" and steamed down the Arkansas river for Little Rock again. I again spent several days in Little Rock when I went aboard another craft for Pine Bluff. I reached this place with only five dollars and no friend or acquaintance to turn to—but I did not despond. I went to the hotel and remained indoors all the evening as it was raining hard and cold. The next day I went out into the streets and made some inquiries about business but all answers to them were unsatisfactory as were all efforts unsuccessful. That night was the gloomiest of my life— just money enough to pay my board and no imployment, no friend. What was to be done. The next morning after breakfast I went to the bar and paid my bill $4.50—and went out into town. I labored incessantly all the morning and failed in every effort. I walked into a confectioner late in the evening and bought 25 cents worth of cakes and ate them eagerly, for I was very hungry. I now had only 25 cents left and went out again determined to beg for work but not for bread! A little before night I met an old man by the name of Keeler (God bless him) and soon contracted with him to work at his Saw Mill (1/2 mile from town) for $15.00 per month. I served in this capacity for three weeks and then taken his wagon and teams and hauled lumber from the mill to town about four months. I then secured a situation of overseer on a farm in the bottoms at $22 1/2 a month. I commenced business with Brownfield (my employer's name) on the 1st of June 1859 and continued with him for one year, when I voluntarily left him, and rejecting other good offers I took the stage for Little Rock once more. I arrived in Washington about the middle of June 1860, and immediately went before a Judge Hubbard, School Commissioner, and stood an examination, received my certificate and went out in quest of a school. I soon succeeded in making up a five months school, which paid me very handsomely and afforded me much pleasure. You may judge with what success my juvenile effort were attended when I inform you that at the earnest solicitation of my patrons I resumed my school the first of the year 1861 in the same settlement for a term of ten months.

I taught until the 15th of July when I left Washington in a volunteer company for the war then raging fiercely in Southern Missouri. I dismissed my school of over forty scholars with tears in my eyes for there were associations to be severed which were both pleasing and agreeable to me. I delighted in the business and loved my scholars and I believe they had an affection for me. But our state was about to be invaded; McCulloch, matchless McCulloch had called and duty was calling long and loud and I had to obey; nor have I ever regretted. I went out as cavalry; was mustered into the Confederate Service on the 4th of August 1861. And passed unscratched through the memorable battle of Oak Hills. I spent that fall on the Kansas border with my regiment—2nd Ark. Cav. commanded by Col. afterwards Gen. John [James] McIntosh. The winter of '61, I was spent in quarters on the Arkansas river, 15 miles below Van Buren. Late in February '62 we were ordered to the front and participated in the battle of Elk Horn. Immediately after this battle we were dismounted and transfered to this side of the river. We had no enjoyment at Corinth as our regiment was on guard duty. From Tuplo we were ordered to Knoxville Tenn. and placed under the command of Gen. E. Kirby Smith. We made the whole tour of Kentucky under this popular leader and fought and won the battle of Richmond under him. I did not participate in the fight being behind the command. We returned from Kentucky by the way of Cumberland Gap and after a few days of rest and recuperation, were thrown in front of Gen Rosenkrantz's Army at Nashville—our line of battle extending in a semicircle around Murfeesboro; where the great battle of 31st Dec 1862 was fought. You know the particulars. After the battle we withdrew to this place where we are likely to remain for sometimes. Now, Gus, you have a brief, connected and true narrative of my life since we parted. Not—very interesting—or eventful one but I trust you may not become weary in its perusal and will favor me with an outline of yours history in return, as I shall confidently expect it.

If I survive this war I will spend a few weeks with my parents and then go to Washington. Hempstead County, Arkansas where I have some business that should be settled, and then I will go over into Texas to see you if you are there at that time. I have never been in Texas and would consequently like to see the country. I don't expect to live in Hempstead County again and do not know where I may locate—but I have often thought of the bottoms of Arkansas river—below where I overseed. Those are the best lands, everything considered that I ever saw and I would delight to make cotton on them. But these speculations are all premature and I will desist. Whenever I become a free man again I will find you Gus, if you are anywhere in these Confederate States.

My success in Arkansas in accumulating money was not very great but quite satisfactory—considering the running around that I done. I am the owner of a small but good tract of land. The several regiments and battalions in our brigade are being consolidated to day. It is almost impossible to get recruits from home to fill out our decimated ranks, hence the necessity of consolidation, and then the officers want to go home. My Captain leaves in a few days for Washington and I will send this by him that far. You must write to me every opportunity you have of sending a letter by hand, for the mails never bring them through. Wishing much happiness and a long life to you and lady. I remain, Gus, your faithful and affectionate friend forever,

Matt

What connects a man, a soldier, like Matt Riddick to Arkansas? Why, Mexico, of course. He was following the lead of his generation and moving to seize the fruits of his nation's conquest.

Matt Riddick was a native of Georgia, educated at a Methodist herbal medicine school in Macon where he developed life-long friendships. He had pledged to one of his companions, Augustus Ball, that they would both head to "The West" and make a new home. Without the Mexican War there simply would have been no *West* to go to. In his letter, Riddick mentions California as his ultimate goal. Without the Mexican War there would have been no California.

Riddick went to Arkansas instead of the more traditional St. Louis because Fort Smith was a more practical gateway to the west, and one that led first to the Colorado Gold Fields, increasingly home to thousands of his fellow Georgians. Arkansas was still a rough-and-tumble frontier, and had only been a state for a generation, so for someone from Georgia, Fort Smith, not Fort Worth, might have been where the west began.

He left Georgia in the first place because of the coming troubles and tension. From 1848 on there had been a growing rift. The spoils of the Mexican War—chiefly land—had exacerbated the issues over who could export their particular American vision to this new real estate. The squabble had led to a heated compromise—of 1850—which brought in places like California as free states. It remained silent as to the rest of the territories. Then, in 1854, the Kansas-Nebraska Act introduced the logically sound but practically stupid concept of Popular Sovereignty. In reality, it was a ticket to civil war in those territories.

There were other issues. A novel entitled *Uncle Tom's Cabin* gave northerners a view of the South in all of its whiskey-soaked, ill-managed, card-playing, and slave-beating glory and hardened the arguments. Slavery, after all, is evil. Slave owners, and those whom tolerate them, must also be evil. The Dredd Scott case moved the Supreme Court into an untenable position by declaring that free soil did not make free men. This idea, of course, is as preposterous now as it was then, and allowed abolitionists to declare that august body as corrupt and contemptuous, and no longer relevant to the debate. Finally, John Brown's Harper's Ferry raid made martyrs of terrorists.

No wonder Matt Riddick wanted to leave Georgia. These intractable issues, he knew, might consume him. He wanted to experience the promise of America that the West seemed to offer. The promise of a God-ordained Manifest Destiny was the same reason that Arkansans cheerfully answered their nation's call for volunteers to conquer the peace in the War with Mexico, and by consequence conquer the West.

To close the cosmic wheel on this particular issue, one must consider the name Archibald Yell. He, after all, commanded the "Rackensackers" in Mexico, and became one of the nation's fallen heroes of the battle of Buena Vista in February 1847. "He received two wounds, either of which was mortal," a witness reported. "One was in the mouth which lance entered crosswise, and was driven entirely through his head, the other was in the breast. He was the most ghastly sight I ever saw."

This rough little battle killed Yell but made two presidents—Zachary Taylor and Jefferson Davis—and a host of heroes. It made a number of generals out of some of the officers present. Artillery Captain Braxton Bragg would go on to lead Confederate troops in the Civil War, as would Colonel Yell's

The U.S. Army relied heavily on its "Flying Artillery" in the war. This artillery lieutenant, wearing a West Point ring, is thought to be Thomas (later "Stonewall") Jackson, who fought around Mexico City. (Courtesy of Dr. William Schultz)

subordinates—James Fleming Fagan, Solon Borland, John Seldon Roane and Albert Pike. Other Mexican War veterans like Thomas C. Hindman and Thomas Churchill would not serve with Arkansans in Mexico. After the war, these blooded warriors moved to the state in the 1850s. They, like the even later-arriving Riddick, would serve with Arkansans in battle, and many would lead a salient role in the great national calamity that lay a dozen years in the future.

It would seem odd, then, for a state that had only recently been added to the Union, and that had bled on behalf of the nation in the Mexican War, to secede. Yet, it did, a cultural and political allegiance to the South sundering the bonds that had once tied it to the United States. When the Civil War did come, a Mexican War veteran, Captain James Totten, commanded the artillery that defended the U.S. Arsenal at Little Rock. His guns, U.S. Model 1842 six-pounder smoothbores, were aimed into the city, but he decided against using them. On Feb. 8, 1861, he surrendered the public property under his care, including these guns, the very ones, it turns out, used by Bragg at Buena Vista and the ones that had supported the advance of Yell's Arkansans on that fateful day.

As these U.S. troops, the last vestige of Federal authority, left Little Rock, they were escorted part of the way out of town by Arkansas militia. Among them was a unit from Helena calling itself the Yell Rifles after the state's greatest war hero up to that time. This was but a dying echo of the Mexican War, the last great national outing, so soon to be drowned in fresh fraternal blood.

Lieutenant George H. Thomas of the Third Artillery was forced to abandon his 6-pounder at Buena Vista. The gun was later recaptured outside Mexico City. (Courtesy of Dr. William Schultz)

Window on the Southwest: Arkansas's Role in the Mexican War

By C. Fred Williams

The Mexican War marked the first turning point in Arkansas's history. Prior to 1848, the state's focus was on the West, but as a result of the war with Mexico Arkansans reversed their perspective and became increasingly attracted to issues and policies held dear by Southern states east of the Mississippi River.[1]

That Arkansas would have a role in the War with Mexico was determined to a large extent when the Territory was formed in 1819. In an ironic sense of timing, the Committee on Territories in the U.S. House of Representatives began hearings on the bill to create Arkansas Territory even as the Executive branch was putting the final touches on the Adams-Onís (Transcontinental) Treaty that defined the nation's boundary between Spanish Mexico and the Louisiana Purchase. Arkansas's western boundary was inextricably tied to the United States' interest in the Southwest. While Spain did not in itself present a major threat to America, it represented a European presence with traditions and alliances to other countries, particularly France, that could threaten U.S. ambitions in the Trans-Mississippi West. Because of those potential dangers America needed a strong, robust presence in this recently acquired region and in 1819 Arkansas represented the nation's commitment to defend its interests. The newly created territory was a sentinel to serve notice to any would-be foreign threat and to provide a window to view the Southwest along a four hundred-mile border.[2]

The background for establishing U. S. dominance in the Trans-Mississippi region began soon after the Treaty of Ghent ended the

War of 1812. With its conflict with Great Britain largely resolved, newly elected President James Monroe turned his attention to hemispheric issues and focused on two areas of disagreement with Spain—Florida and Texas. Each involved a boundary question that had been in contention for almost a decade. Florida, on the basis of proximity, carried more immediate political weight because of slaveholders' influence in Congress. However, the Texas "question" presented more long-term problems for the nation and had direct implications for Arkansas.[3]

President Monroe picked John Quincy Adams to provide the leadership for this revived interest in the border. Fresh from his ambassadorial duties at the Court of Saint James, Adams returned from England in the summer of 1817 and assumed the reins of the State Department on Sept. 21. As one of his first actions, he contacted Spain's Ambassador Don Luis de Onís and indicated his interest in continuing negotiations on boundaries between the two countries.[4] He placed Texas at the top of the negotiating agenda and indicated that the U. S. was willing to adjust his position from the Rio Grande River as the western-most boundary of the Louisiana Territory to

Even as Arkansas was becoming a territory in 1819, Secretary of State John Quincy Adams was negotiating a treaty with Spain that made Texas's status contentious in the United States for decades. (Courtesy of the Library of Congress Prints and Photographs Division)

the Colorado River, some three hundred miles to the east in the central part of the province. When Onís pointed out that Monroe, as Secretary of State in the James Madison administration, had been willing to negotiate with the Sabine River, another three hundred miles further east, as the eastern boundary between Spanish and American territories, Adams countered that times had changed. Not only had the United States signed an agreement with Great Britain (Rush-Bagot, 1816) but the Russian government had also pulled back its claims in the Pacific Northwest, leaving the U.S. in a better position to expand its interests farther west.[5]

President Andrew Jackson died before the war began, but was a proponent of Texas annexation. "Extend the Area of Freedom," a paraphrase of Jackson, was sewn on one Little Rock company flag. (Courtesy of the Library of Congress Prints and Photographs Division)

The Adams-Onís discussions on Texas were still in preliminary stages when Gen. Andrew Jackson, commander of the Southern District of the U.S. Army, launched a military raid into Florida. This "Florida incident" became a major controversy in the Monroe administration and also had major implications for Arkansas. It forced Adams to re-focus on Florida and expend considerable energy in defending Jackson's actions. In short, Jackson's Florida raid caused Adams to abandon claims to a larger part of Texas in exchange for secure control over territory east of the Mississippi River. He was willing to trade Texas for Florida.[6]

Early in 1818 Adams indicated a willingness to accept the Sabine River as the east-west dividing line between the Louisiana Territory and Texas. He then spent most of the summer and fall trying to resolve the northern border between the two countries. By October he had settled on a plan that extended a border from the Sabine to the Red River, followed that river west to the 100th Meridian, then north to the Arkansas River following that stream to its head waters, where the proposed boundary turned north again to the 42nd Parallel and followed that latitude west to the Pacific Ocean. Onís ultimately accepted his line of demarcation and the two diplomats signed a formal agreement that solidified the boundaries on Feb. 22, 1819.[7]

The Committee on Territories took up the Arkansas territorial bill just as Adams and Onís were reaching closure on their negotiations. Committee members were aware of the new boundary and in partial consequence of that treaty, the committee fixed Arkansas's southern boundary as extending from the 33rd Parallel to the Red River, then west along the Red to the 100th Meridian in keeping with the boundaries agreed to in the Adams-Onís Treaty. The full House of Representatives accepted this recommendation and voted to admit the new Arkansas Territory into the family on March 4. The newest addition to the nation occupied a huge land mass, more than 100,000 square miles, on the Southwest frontier just across the Red River from Spanish-controlled Texas. Neither Spain, nor her European allies, could doubt the commitment the United States was making to the Trans-Mississippi region.[8]

Less than a year after the southern/northern boundary for the Louisiana Purchase had been settled, two other historic events converged and re-oriented the Monroe administration's thinking about Arkansas and the Southwest. The first event came in Mexico where provincial rebels joined a decade-long revolt coming out of South America to overthrow Spanish colonial rule and established an independent government. This new "Republic of Mexico" was hardly in position to challenge the U.S. presence in the Trans-Mississippi and greatly reduced the need for Monroe and Adams to flex their diplomatic muscle along the Red River.[9]

The second event to alter policy in the Trans-Mississippi had to do with Indian policy. Apparently a key factor in Thomas Jefferson's decision to accept the Louisiana Purchase was his thinking on how it might affect U.S. relations with the Native American population. One idea was to create a "Red Nation" west of the Mississippi River, an Indian Territory that would separate the native population from the encroaching Anglo Americans until the two groups could reach some type of accommodation and, at least in Jefferson's view, be assimilated.[10]

Beginning in 1817, the Monroe administration moved to implement a new Indian policy in the form of the Indian Relocation Act. Under terms of this policy, tribes living east of the Mississippi River were encouraged to voluntarily exchange their homelands for new lands in the west. Indian response to this "offer" was limited, although a significant number of Cherokee, as well as some Shawnee and Delaware, did begin migrating west. A portion of the Cherokee Nation actually signed a formal treaty with the United States on Oct. 18, 1817. Giving up claims in Georgia, about one third of the tribe accepted new lands lying between the Arkansas and White Rivers approximately two hundred miles upstream from their confluence with the Mississippi. These "reservation" lands were still unsurveyed, but appeared well inside the still-undetermined boundaries of the Louisiana Purchase.[11]

The relocating Cherokee were greatly resented by the resident Osage Nation who claimed hunting rights to the land assigned in the Treaty. Within days after the first Cherokee moved into the new reservation, the two tribes engaged in violent conflict and Congress was forced to establish a new military outpost in the Louisiana Purchase. Ostensibly to maintain order between the Cherokee and Osage, the new fort also represented a U.S. commitment to Anglo settlers who were rapidly claiming the region too, even as the Indians relocated. It also alerted Spanish officials about U.S. intent in the region. The installation, commissioned as Fort Smith, was completed in late December 1817, at the confluence of the Poteau and Arkansas Rivers, approximately 400 miles upstream from the Mississippi.[12]

Progress with the Relocation policy was slow, due in part to the imprecise boundary between U.S. and Spanish territory. The Adams-Onís Treaty settled that confusion and in early 1820 President Monroe, through Secretary of War John Calhoun, returned to the Relocation principle. Among the tribes Calhoun sought out, the Choctaw were most amenable to a land exchange and on Oct. 18, 1820, U.S. officials signed the Treaty of Doak's Stand with representatives of the Choctaw Nation. The Treaty gave the Choctaw an enormous amount of land between the Arkansas and Red Rivers, south of the Cherokee reservation, extending west to the 100th Meridian.[13]

Officials in the newly minted Arkansas Territory, and more specifically the editor of the *Arkansas Gazette*, vigorously protested the Choctaw assignment. William Woodruff claimed there were "several thousand" white settlers already living in the lands "given away" to the Choctaw and accused the Monroe administration of turning Arkansas into a "Botany Bay."[14] Clearly, officials in Washington were working at cross purposes. Congress's efforts at creating the large Arkansas Territory in March 1819 was now off-set by the Executive branch reducing the size of that Territory by more than 50 percent through its treaty making powers under the Constitution. That few in Congress were disturbed by the re-orientation of diplomacy in the Trans-Mississippi region was primarily because Spain's influence had been diminished and the lawmakers were not concerned about a threat from Mexico, at least not in 1820.

For a decade after 1820 officials in Washington toyed with the Indian relocation policy and met limited success. The protracted struggle between the Cherokee and Osage, not resolved until 1824, and even then followed by an uneasy truce, was complicated by Mexico's delay in ratifying the Adams-Onís Treaty. However the strong protest by Arkansans to the Relocation policy finally prompted Washington to act. In the closing days of the Monroe Administration, federal negotiators met with Choctaw leaders and renegotiated the Treaty of Doak's Stand. The new Treaty of 1825, signed on Jan. 20, moved the Choctaw boundary farther west to a line beginning "one hundred paces east of ... Fort Smith" south to the Red River.[15] By accepting this agreement, Arkansas moved the Choctaw beyond the "settled" areas in the region, but they also gave up over half the original Territory.[16] Three years later the Cherokee agreed to relocate their original reservation west of a line running north from Fort Smith to the Missouri Border. Ironically, these two Indian tribes now served as the first line in "frontier defense," a role originally intended for Arkansas.[17]

In 1830 the United States government changed its Indian Policy from voluntary relocation to forced resettlement. In that year Congress passed the Indian Removal Act and under the prodding of President Andrew Jackson resettlement of the eastern tribes began in earnest. To complement the removal policy, Congress also passed the Indian Intercourse Act in 1834 that formally recognized an "Indian Country," although without precise boundaries, and granted individual tribes autonomy over their internal affairs.[18] By 1835 more than 30,000 Indians had been removed and that number grew to more than 60,000 by 1840— almost one third of these new residents were on the Arkansas and Missouri borders.

Trading "relocation" for "removal" was not an easy transition. Not only did the forced action create resentment among the tribes toward the United States, but also the reunion of some of the tribesmen, particularly in the Cherokee Nation, was not a happy occasion. Those Cherokee who relocated under the 1817 policy had almost two decades to solidify their holdings and were well established by the time the balance of the tribe arrived in the new territory. Known as the Western Cherokee, they functioned as an autonomous unit separate from their Eastern tribesmen.[19]

Cherokee internal affairs were further complicated when only a minority of the tribe accepted the new removal policy. In 1835, sub-chiefs John and Major Ridge, Elias Boudinot and Stand Watie, representing clans that made up a small minority of the Cherokee nation, signed a treaty with the U.S. government accepting removal. This "Treaty Party," or "Ridge Party," immediately became the object of scorn to the rest of the nation led by Principal Chief John Ross. A blood feud between the Ridge and Ross parties evolved into a full civil war soon after the nation was resettled in Indian Territory.[20]

The Indian "problem" was only one issue facing the U.S. Army in the 1830s. Continued political instability in Mexico made it difficult for that nation to maintain a consistent foreign policy and U.S. diplomats became increasingly frustrated with delays and unresponsive action from their neighbor to the south. For example, as previously mentioned, Mexico was slow in reaffirming the boundary established by the Adams-Onís Treaty; neither did the new government readily agree to a reciprocal trade treaty, nor respond in a timely manner to the mounting claims for property damages filed by U.S. citizens. The Texas revolt in 1836 was only "salt in the wound" for two countries already in a rapidly deteriorating relationship.[21]

The potential trouble with Mexico, particularly if that government moved to align with Indian leaders disgruntled with the U.S. Removal policy, caused federal officials to pay more attention to the southwestern frontier. As when the Lewis and Clark expedition drew national attention to the northwest, officials in the Jackson administration now saw the Red River region for its strategic importance.[22]

Signs of this new interest in the southwest began in early 1832 when Congress passed legislation adding the Arkansas River to the nation's strategic system. The bill provided $15,000 to clear snags and debris from the waterway and also authorized the construction arm of the War Department (soon to become the Corps of Engineers) to "maintain a channel on the Arkansas River." President Jackson signed the bill into law after vetoing a similar measure in 1830. This funding allowed the Arkansas to join the Ohio, Mississippi, and Missouri rivers as part of the nation's infrastructure for providing national defense.[23]

Following up on the legislative mandate, War Department officials assigned Henry M. Shreve, captain of a steamboat detail charged with keeping the vital river channels open, to work on the Arkansas. He arrived at the mouth of the river in August 1833 and removed 20 snags before low water forced him to suspend operations. Returning in January 1834, he worked for six weeks to clear the channel up to Little Rock. On Feb. 22, he noted that in the 250 miles from the mouth of the river he had "removed 1,537 snags" from the channel and had cut another "3,370 snags and logs" from dry sandbars and under the banks in the river bends—an average of almost 200 obstructions, or potential obstructions, per mile.[24]

Obviously, Shreve's work did not eliminate the risk, but it temporarily reduced the hazards and, equally important to the military, it reduced travel time. In 1830 it typically took a steamer more than two weeks to reach New Orleans but by 1840 that time had been reduced to four or five days. More importantly Shreve's work signaled steamboat operators that the Arkansas was now in the system for continued maintenance.

A further indication of the southwest's growing importance came in 1836 when the War Department moved to build an arsenal in Little Rock. The decision was made with the recognition that Little Rock was a gateway to the western frontier, not only a key supply station between the Mississippi River and Indian Territory, but also a portal to Mexico. The city offered the best opportunity to forward position military supplies in anticipation of future trouble. Plans to build the arsenal began in the spring of 1836 when project manager Lieut. F. L. Jones came to Little Rock and selected thirty-six acres in the original town site for the new military installation. Compared to other military bases the Arsenal was small. However, the finished complex included a barracks for enlisted men, officers' quarters, a series of gun repair shops, storage facilities to house 100 tons of ordnance, all done at a cost of $100,000. The ammunition for both small arms and artillery arrived in Little Rock on May 15, 1838, and the installation was formally commissioned on June 23. The facility represented a substantial long-term investment in the region and allowed frontier posts to be re-supplied in a timely manner.[25]

Arkansas was not the only beneficiary of this new military spending. The growing Indian population west of the 95th Meridian and the increasing number of conflicts between resident and removed tribesmen convinced Congress that it must provide better support for the army. The House Committee on Military Affairs as early as 1836 noted:

> The savage tribes which border upon our settlements, from the Canada line to Louisiana, are more dangerous to the lives and property of our citizens than the whole civilized world .... The late sufferings from the Black Hawk war in the north, and the more recent barbarities of the Florida Indians in the south admonish us of the necessity of furnishing more effectual protection to our inland borders.[26]

It was this heightened concern that caused army engineers to begin the groundwork to allow quicker and better access to the frontier, and the quartermaster department to initiate plans to stockpile supplies closer to the western border. Army field commanders also took steps to reposition troops in the region. In late spring 1836 Gen. Edmund P. Gaines, from his command center for the Department of the West in Lexington, Kentucky, prepared to move six companies of infantry and two companies of dragoons to Fort Towson on the Red River. The dragoons were new to the army organization, having been authorized by Congress in 1834 after previous attempts at creating a Ranger Division in the Western Army failed due to limited participation and inadequate funding.[27]

The growing number of mounted troops indicated a changing strategy among military planners. The increased population in the Trans-Mississippi region, both red and white, forced both Congress and the Executive branch to re-think plans for the western territory. Only a thin line of frontier forts separated more than 60,000 Indians from perhaps twice that many white settlers along a front that stretched more than a thousand miles from Louisiana to Minnesota. As an indication of how sparse the Army's resources were, in 1837 the Western Command had approximately 7,000 troops under its supervision distributed among nine forts and support stations. Fort Gibson, some forty miles west of the Arkansas border, was the largest of these installations with 491 men followed by Fort Leavenworth on the Missouri River in Kansas with 431 men. The smallest, Fort Jessup near the Sabine River in Louisiana, had 331 enlisted men and officers. Clearly the Army was understaffed to handle the potential Indian threat that could also be complicated by problems with Mexico.[28]

To best utilize its limited personnel, War Department officials decided to build a north-south road connecting the Red and Missouri Rivers and ultimately continuing above the Missouri to the Mississippi River in Minnesota Territory. The proposed road was projected to connect existing military posts, although in some instances it would require that new facilities be built at strategic locations. The brainchild of Secretary of War Lewis Cass, the Secretary justified the route on the basis that the Indian Intercourse Act of 1834 obligated the United States to protect individual tribes from inter-tribal conflict and from intrusion by aggressive whites who refused to recognize Indian sovereignty. Providing this protection would require rapid deployment and a high state of readiness on the part of the Western Command in order to ensure "a speedy concentration of troops" in troubled areas. Cass suggested that "a strong strike force of dragoons" be positioned at opposite ends of the road and a third detachment stationed near the middle of the route. In addition, by establishing such a road the U.S. government would define an east-west boundary between Indian Territory and the "sovereign states" in the Trans-Mississippi region.[29]

Cass's proposal was championed in the U.S. Senate by Thomas Hart Benton of Missouri. Benton pointed out that the United States had failed to develop a comprehensive Indian policy and said it was time "a systematic plan for protection of our frontiers ... [be] devised and adopted."[30] Cass supported the Senator's comments by pointing out that the problem would only get worse as Indian removal progressed. He reminded lawmakers of the danger poised by the Plains Indians, saying "all of them are roaming in their habits and the nature of the country, as well as the general possession of horses, enables them to extend their war excursions to great distances."[31]

Congress approved Cass's "frontier defense plan," as the proposal became known, on July 2, 1836. The bill carried with it a $100,000 appropriation "to construct a road from Fort Towson on the Red River to a place on the Missouri River between the St. Peters and Des Moines Rivers." All military posts west of that road were to be relocated along its eastern right of way.[32]

Creating the frontier defense line gave Arkansas's congressional delegation an opportunity to re-open the question of re-commissioning Fort Smith.[33] As previously mentioned, Arkansans had never been satisfied with the War Department's decision to close Fort Smith in favor of a new post, Fort Gibson, deeper in Indian Territory. However, as a Territory the people of Arkansas had limited influence in Congress and their delegate Henry W. Conway was unable to prevent the closure in 1825. But circumstances changed over the next decade. Not only did Arkansas gain statehood in June 1836, and thus substantially increase its political presence in Washington, but as also noted, Indian policy had changed. The increased number of Indians on Arkansas's border and the mounting incidents of violent crimes gave Senator Ambrose Sevier and Senator William Fulton the leverage needed to re-open the Fort Smith issue. In 1838 the Senators announced that the War Department was re-commissioning Fort Smith and construction on the new facility, located in the same vicinity as the first post, would begin within the year.[34]

Construction on the "second Fort Smith" did begin in early 1839 but it was not completely finished until 1846 due to inconsistent funding and lack of skilled workers. However the fort's influence as a supply station began to be felt almost immediately. The Quartermaster Department began stockpiling supplies at a temporary camp near the construction site to be trans-shipped to other posts along the military road. Local land owner John Rogers began to plat a new town, also called Fort Smith, a short distance from the fort and did a flourishing business selling town lots.[35]

The new Fort Smith was highly controversial among military leaders. However, less than three months after work on the post began, civil strife among the Cherokee broke out again with such brutality that Arkansas's political leaders felt vindicated in their instance that the new fort be built. The Cherokee civil war stemmed from the internal divisions the tribe went through during the removal process. Soon after the last "official" group arrived in Indian Territory in late 1838, John Ross summoned representatives from all members of the tribe to his new residence at Park Hill, just outside Tahlequah. After three days of feasting and speech making, he asked for a truce among the three factions. Each group, the "old settlers" from the 1817 Treaty, the group who signed the "new, or pretend, Treaty" in 1835, and the Ross or National Party who had refused to sign any treaty but were removed nevertheless, agreed to re-unite as a nation.[36]

The pledge of loyalty lacked commitment and in early June 1839, members of the Ross Party launched a coordinated attack against the four principal signers of the 1835 treaty. Within hours Major Ridge, John Ridge and Elias Boudinot were ambushed and assassinated. Stand Waite was spared only because a change in plans caused him to alter his route and thus avoid his planned attackers.[37] As news of the killings spread through the nation, loyalists to the Ridge Party retaliated against the Ross Party. A full-scale civil war ensued as each faction looted, killed, and burned property of the other. To calm the disturbances, Principal Chief Ross formed a "Light Horse" police force, but individuals appointed to this force served more to terrorize their opponents than to keep order.[38]

Both sides in the Cherokee civil war appealed to Gen. Mathew Arbuckle, newly appointed commander of the Second Military Department at Fort Smith, for help. Arbuckle appealed to both factions to respect their pledge for a truce but calm was not restored before more than a dozen people were killed and thousands of dollars in property was damaged or destroyed.[39]

In 1845, the conflict between the Cherokee factions flared again along a 100-mile front along the tribe's western border from the Arkansas River to the Missouri-Kansas Border. Arbuckle responded with a major show of force that demonstrated the effectiveness of Lewis Cass's frontier defense plan. Summoning a dragoon detachment from Fort Gibson, he assigned the mounted troops to occupy strategic positions along the Cherokee-Arkansas border. By April 1846 most of the conflict was under control but again the war took its toll. Arbuckle reported thirty-four people killed but did not put a dollar amount on property damage.[40]

Ironically, just as Gen. Arbuckle was bringing order to the Cherokee civil war, events in Texas launched the Mexican War. On April 24 Mexican Gen. Mariano Arista ordered 1,600 troops across the Rio Grande River to engage American forces under the command of Gen. Zachary Taylor. On May 11, President James K. Polk used this skirmish to ask Congress for a declaration of war against Mexico. For the next eighteen months more than 1,500 Arkansans were involved in the nation's most successful war, based on territorial acquisition. But as important as the war was for the Nation, it had even more implications for Arkansas. The war eliminated the "Indian threat" by freeing the U.S. Army to focus on Native Americans without concern for other foreign foes. Two decades after the Mexican conflict, the U.S. abandoned the concept of Indian Territory and moved to a concentration policy. In the twin treaties of Medicine Lodge (1867) and Fort Laramie (1868), federal officials reduced the "great reservation" into two small reservations identified today as Oklahoma and South Dakota under the watchful eye of a larger, more vigilant military. Arkansans no longer worried about an Indian uprising on the western border.

The war also ended the political careers of Archibald Yell and Ambrose Sevier, the state's two most influential politicians. Yell was killed at the battle of Buena Vista and Sevier gave up his Senate seat to help negotiate terms for ending the war. Not only did his "Peace Commission" arrive too late for meaningful input in the settlement, but when he returned to Arkansas his colleagues failed to honor his request to regain his old position. He died a broken man after a quarter century of public service.

Perhaps the biggest change of all, however, was the war served to, if not close, at least shutter the state's window on the Southwest and reverse its perspective from west to east. The decade following the war a plantation economy overshadowed the subsistence, self-sufficient lifestyle that had characterized Arkansas for three decades. The federal census in 1850 revealed that for the first time the lowland counties had overtaken the upland counties in population. Cotton and slaves replaced Indians and violence as the dominant political issues and a region that had grown up looking to Washington for support and believing in "manifest destiny" now turned inward and relied on state's rights and popular sovereignty.

Before the war, Arkansas was on the American frontier. "Manifest Destiny" had long been a phrase that encouraged expansion into the West. (Courtesy of the University of Texas at Arlington, Special Collections Library)

Rackensack in the Field:
Arkansans in the U.S.-Mexican War

By William A. Frazier

The U.S.-Mexican War goes largely unnoticed by most of the American public. Many Americans confuse it with the Spanish-American War, if they are aware at all that another conflict other than the Civil War happened in the nineteenth century. For Arkansas, this may be for the best. In the various histories of the war, the state's reputation has been fairly tarnished.

While the first soldiers who joined the military for the war with Mexico sought honor and glory, the Arkansas troops who came home must have been frustrated in this goal.[1] What is generally acknowledged of Arkansans' involvement in the war is that its volunteers were so poorly trained and badly disciplined as to be nicknamed the "Mounted Devils." Perhaps it is known that one of the state's regiment, called the Mounted Gunmen, ran ingloriously from the field of battle at Buena Vista. Maybe it is known that a portion of the Arkansas Regiment was taken prisoner at Encarnacíon without firing a shot because it had posted few or no pickets. Just as likely, it might be known that some of the most notorious atrocities committed during the conflict were at the hands of Arkansans. These are the bits of history most likely to be connected with Arkansas's troops in any large narrative of the war. There is no indication but that all of them are true.

Still, there is more to know of Arkansas troops in the war than a handful of shameful incidents. All of the soldiers of the Regiment of Mounted Gunmen were not a source of dishonor for the state. There are other Arkansans who served beyond the regiment, some with distinction. Rather than try to account for a complete narrative of Arkansans, a quick survey of the life that most Arkansas soldiers lived and some accounting of their biggest battles is in order.

The Troops

Arkansans were involved in almost every battle of the war at one level or another. But who were the Arkansas troops? Defining Arkansans then as we would in the twenty-first century now is hardly appropriate. In the 1840s, many young men who joined the ranks as Arkansans had not been born in the state. Perhaps their families had settled in the state when they were children, or perhaps before they were soldiers they had traveled to the state themselves, and were subsequently viewed as Arkansans. The military force the state produced was a mixture of men from many points east, although the majority had families who had come from Kentucky, Tennessee, the Carolinas and other Southern states. They were viewed by their peers as Arkansans, nonetheless.

From the standpoint of quantifying the Arkansans involved, it is safe to say that about fifteen hundred Arkansas soldiers served in various companies. Approximately half of those, about 870, were enrolled in the Regiment of Mounted Gunmen. Another 380 were in the Arkansas Battalion, an infantry unit bound for the Indian Territory. The next highest figure was a series of companies. Captain Stephen B. Enyart's Company of mounted men had about seventy five men from northwest Arkansas and served along the Rio Grande in 1847 and 1848 after the fighting had ended there. The Twelfth Infantry companies of Captains Allen Wood and J. Banks Anthony may have put as many as one hundred Arkansans in the army as regulars, although some portion of those men had served previously as volunteers in either the Regiment of Mounted

Gunmen or the battalion of infantry. Another company, referred to sometimes as Meares's Buena Vista Cavalry, also contained a majority of Arkansans. Most of the Arkansas soldiers in Meares's company served in the Arkansas Regiment of Mounted Gunmen and were re-enlisted, although some number of them may have been teamsters or other civilian contractors from Arkansas and some re-enlisted from other states' regiments serving in the vicinity of Saltillo, Mexico. After that, the numbers scattered throughout the regulars is difficult to ascertain, but there is information available on some regular army officers.[2]

While six hundred or seven hundred men saw service outside the Mounted Gunmen, that is the largest body of troops sent into service and those 870 men are worth some specific attention. The regiment was recruited in May and June 1846 and the companies were mustered mostly at Washington, Arkansas, but also at Van Buren and Ozark. While patriotism and the fervor to join the military at the outbreak of the war were motivators for recruits, it is easy to underestimate just how much politics figured into the recruiting process. Many, if not all, of the men who organized companies had political ambitions. A great number of men were recruited at political meetings under way in the summer of 1846. A Whig meeting in Little Rock snagged thirty-five recruits, for example, as Captain Albert Pike hoisted his company flag in front of the Anthony Hotel to lure in prospects.[3] Although the majority of Arkansans were Jackson/Polk Democrats, a significant number were Whigs. One of the state's most prominent Whigs, Pike was captain of a company from Pulaski County. Since Whigs in the state tended to be in the cities or among the biggest plantations along the rivers, it is no surprise that the Phillips County company—which likely had a significant number of Whigs, as well—was put under Pike's command as part of the two-company squadron.

The officers of the companies initially were elected by the men, and were replaced through new elections as needed because of attrition by disease or death. Thus, men aspiring to be even mere sergeants had to have the respect and admiration of those in his company. Being a taskmaster, obviously, would not get a man moved up in the ranks. Nor would it serve him well in his political ambitions after the war. This made it unlikely that a volunteer officer, commissioned or not, was going to be a strict disciplinarian. The men under an officer's command were not just his soldiers; hopefully, they were his constituents and required a slightly more delicate treatment than did those in the regular army.

When it was announced in the Arkansas newspapers in the spring of 1846 that the state was to raise a regiment for Mexico and a battalion for the Indian Territory, Solon Borland, the state's adjutant general, made it clear that companies would be taken on a first-come basis. The first ten companies to be either mustered in by regular officers or to report to the rendezvous at Washington, Arkansas, were to be accepted into the Mounted Gunmen. Pulaski County enrolled two companies, and one each came from Crawford, Franklin, Independence, Johnson, Phillips, Pope and Sevier counties. Another company was composed of men from Saline and Hot Spring counties. Com-

Solon Borland, a physician and newspaper editor, was elected the Arkansas Regiment's major. He was captured during a patrol south of Saltillo and held as a prisoner of war before escaping as U.S. troops neared Mexico City in 1847. (Courtesy of the Library of Congress Prints and Photographs Division)

panies were organized in Searcy, Ouachita and Jackson counties, but were not mustered. The Washington County company under Captain Stephen B. Enyart reached Washington in 1846 without being accepted. Enyart's men were provisioned for the march home, but they did not leave happily.[4]

Governor Thomas Drew's call for troops specifically defined the number of men to be in each company of the Mounted Gunmen. There was a captain, a first lieutenant, a second lieutenant, four sergeants, four corporals, two buglers and one man whose duties included work as a farrier and blacksmith. There were to be 78 men per company, 64 of whom were to be privates. But the numbers fluctuated by company.[5]

The regiment elected its officers on July 4, 1846, at Washington, Arkansas, and there was significant politicking for the various positions. All indications are that Captain Pike of Pulaski County desired the colonel's position, but his Whig politics made it unlikely he could garner the necessary votes among a regiment predominately of Democrats. A private who had joined the ranks of Captain Borland's Pulaski County company, however, campaigned for the job from the moment he left Little Rock until the election. Arkansas's only congressman, Archibald Yell, had fallen in with the men like a regular soldier—even if he was

Archibald Yell left his seat in the U.S. House of Representatives in 1846 to volunteer as a private in the Arkansas Regiment, but the former governor was soon elected the regiment's colonel. (Courtesy of the Old State House Museum)

The "Try Us" battle flag of the "Van Buren Avengers" was among the company flags used by the Arkansas Regiment. (Courtesy of the Old State House Museum)

sharing a tent with Captain Borland. The former governor was an easy choice to the position, since he had fought with Andrew Jackson in the War of 1812 and in Indian wars afterward. For lieutenant colonel, the regiment elected John Seldon Roane, captain of the "Van Buren Avengers" and the state's former speaker of the house. Fiery newspaperman and doctor Solon Borland was chosen as major. The other significant regimental position was that of adjutant and went to Gaston Meares, a Lafayette County attorney who had attended though had not completed his studies at West Point. It was the most significant formal military training in the regiment and went largely unused.[6]

The regiment was poorly outfitted from the start. Upon leaving Little Rock, Captain Borland may have owned the only tent belonging to his company. Some supplies were available at Washington for the rendezvous. But the Arkansas troops' arms and some other supplies had been mistakenly shipped to Fort Smith. It was months before the equipment caught up with the troops at San Antonio, where they were first ordered by Gen. John Ellis Wool, a regular who was to be the Arkansans' commanding officer and had at one time served as Inspector General of the Army. As such, Wool was a stickler for detail and Yell's men drove him to distraction; Wool once wrote that Yell's men were "wholly without instruction and Colonel Yell is determined to leave them in that condition."[7]

In fact, some of the men had been training all along the way. The core of Pike's company was composed of a militia company, the Little Rock Guards, and had hoped to enter the army as the newly famed "flying artillery." But when Pike's company could only be accepted as mounted troops for combat, he began to train them as soon as possible, as did Capt. John Preston of the Phillips County company. Those two companies—largely from around Little Rock and Helena—were to later compose the best-trained squadron from the Arkansas Regiment, and fought under the command of the Dragoons, or regular cavalry, during the battle of Buena Vista.

But the assumption that the rest of the Arkansas troops were wholly untrained may be inaccurate. Dragoon Sam Chamberlain mentions training the Arkansans in carbine and saber use.[8] Sergeant Jonathon H. Buhoup of Captain Danley's Company, in his account of the Arkansas Regiment, notably describes their training as foot soldiers while at San Antonio: "The different corps were daily employed in drilling—it had indeed the appearance of a Military Academy."[9] Drill not only served as instruction for troops, but served to break the tedium of camp life and kept idle volunteers out of trouble while at any lengthy bivouac.

Among the volunteers' responsibilities along the march was taking care of their horses. The animals had to be fed, watered and brushed before the soldiers could worry about getting food and rest. One soldier described his frustrations at spending days trying to take care of a sick horse while the army was still on the march.

A lot of horses died along the way. Other soldiers had horses stolen by locals as they got deeper into Mexico. The combined effect was that a significant number of men were left afoot or bouncing along in teamsters' wagons until they could buy what they considered inferior mounts in Mexico, a troubling situation for horse soldiers.[10]

A CAMP WASHING DAY.

Arkansas troops in the volunteer regiment performed a variety of tasks. After a long day in the saddle, setting up camp, tending horses, cooking, washing clothes and standing guard were among their responsibilities. (Courtesy of the Library of Congress Prints and Photographs Division)

A significant amount of time out of the saddle was devoted to food preparation. The protocol of the mess was decided by company, some opting for several smaller messes, others choosing maybe two large messes. The rations were supposed to be three-fourths pounds of beef or pork per day, but it seldom lived up to that quantity and the quality was equally troubling: "The beef we here received was very bad—so poor, as the soldiers say, that to throw it against a smooth plank it would stick."[11] Morning meals were prepared the night before to guarantee the soldiers could get moving early, but it also came with the danger of being stolen. Sergeant Buhoup's account describes a near mutiny as food came to be at a premium and the men were issued nine ears of corn each in lieu of bread.[12] Each company of men was also issued a hand-cranked mill, but it the men clearly preferred to not use it for more than their coffee. The Arkansas soldiers also supplemented their food with what was available in Mexico. Yams, hot chocolate, and blocks of sugar were among the items bought from the locals. There are references by soldiers, too, of the Arkansans stealing apples, sugar cane and even cattle from locals at various times along the march, but generally they seem to have not suffered much for food.[13]

Such was not the case, however, with water. The deeper the Arkansans marched into Mexico, the more problems they had getting water in decent quantity and quality. One indication was that some teamsters were keeping water casks on their wagons and charging the troopers for a drink.[14] Another was that issues over water ultimately led to the regiment's officers being arrested by General Wool. Upon leaving San Antonio, Wool had decided that the Arkansans would bivouac on the east side of the camp. As each camp was set up at a water supply, it was not a problem when the water was in a well or tank. But when the water was flowing, the easternmost camp tended to be on the downstream side of the river or creek headed as it flowed east toward the Gulf of Mexico. With about 1,500 men—soldiers and teamsters, included—and hundreds of horses and stock animals nearby, downstream was a septic location from which to be drawing water. After some protests, Colonel Yell made the decision on Dec. 1, 1846, to not camp where assigned after a march, moving instead to another nearby stream. When General Wool learned of this, he ordered Yell to move his men to their assigned position. Yell refused and was put under arrest. Command of the Arkansans devolved to Lieutenant Colonel Roane, who likewise refused and was arrested. When a sergeant was sent with orders to Major Borland to assume the command and follow the orders, Borland took offense that an officer had dared to send a noncommissioned officer with an order, and had the sergeant arrested and sent back to Wool; in his turn Borland, too, was arrested. Command after this incident devolved to the senior officer in the regiment, Capt. Andrew Porter of Independence County, who carried out the orders with mixed approval from the Arkansas troops. For some days, Yell, Roane and Borland were forced to ride at the rear of the line of march. Eventually, Wool came to some accommodation that allowed the Arkansas officers to rejoin their command. Until this incident, the Arkansans barely viewed themselves as a single unit, identifying themselves more with the county their Company represented. State loyalty in the 1840s seems to have been a fairly nebulous concept for men drawn from all over the South. While there were exceptions, the men generally appreciated their regimental officers, Arkansas officers, for coming to their defense. It gave the regiment a sense of cohesion that it had not seen before the confrontation.[15]

Almost from the moment that the Arkansas Mounted Gunmen mustered at Washington, their health was a problem. A number of the men who tried to enlist at Washington were turned away because they were not up to the standards expected of men facing life in the saddle for hundreds of miles. Consequently, some individuals from companies not accepted into the regiment filled the ranks of companies depleted by this elimination of manpower.[16] Riding from southwest Arkansas toward Shreveport and on to San Antonio in July took its toll. A significant number of men in San Antonio turned for home due to illness, while some died there. So many were ill, in fact, that Solon Borland was left to tend to the sick in San Antonio as General Wool's column left the city for the Rio Grande in September 1846.[17] A combination of unwholesome food, water that was often stagnant and insufficient, a climb into the mountains in Mexico and the change in seasons took its toll on the Arkansans. A measles outbreak—a troublesome disease under the best of circumstances in the nineteenth century—became more dangerous in cold weather. The fever that accompanied the measles combined with the common cold to kill some soldiers.[18] The Arkansas Regiment did not leave the state unattended: Dr. Craven Peyton was the regimental surgeon and had two assistants. Borland, a physician in Little Rock, likely helped some.[19]

Beyond the Arkansas Regiment, the most serious health concern for troops in Mexico was the feared *vomito negro* (yellow fever) in the tropical areas around Vera Cruz. Gen. Winfield Scott, in his invasion plans for that city, had tried desperately to gain a foothold in February 1847 rather than allow his men to suffer the ravages of that disease in the warmer months. Although his troops landed March 9 and the siege was over three weeks later, some troops had to be left to garrison the city. Among those was Col. Louis D. Wilson, who had been in charge of the Twelfth Infantry. The yellow fever eventually killed Wilson, and combined with other injuries, led to at least a battalion of the Twelfth's command devolving to Capt. Allen Wood of Carroll County, Arkansas, during the battles of Contreras and Churubusco.[20]

Obviously, not all the soldiers who left for Mexico came home. Most who died there did not have their remains shipped to the United States. Certainly, most high-ranking officers' bodies were shipped back, but they were the exception. In the case of the Arkansans, at least eighteen lost their lives at Buena Vista. A considerably larger unknown number died along the way of disease. Of these, it is known of only four bodies that were shipped back to their homes, three officers and one private. Chief among the officers was Yell, whose body was disinterred in Mexico, sent in a charcoal-lined casket to Little Rock to lay in state at what is today the Old State House Museum, and eventually buried in Fayetteville. Two other officers were also disinterred and reburied in Arkansas, Capt. Andrew Porter and Lt. Erastus B. Strong. Strong, of St. Francis County, was killed in 1847 at the battle of Molino del Rey. The only enlisted man known to have his remains returned to Arkansas was Priv. John B. Pelham of Capt. C. C. Danley's Pulaski County Company.[21]

The Massacre

Understanding how Arkansas troops could have been involved in war atrocities against Mexican civilians requires some perspective on the events that led up to them. Arkansas's Mounted Regiment arrived at Agua Nueva, Mexico, some twenty miles south of Saltillo, in late December 1846. Wool's forces were summoned erroneously to meet Gen. Antonio López de Santa Anna's Mexican army, which in fact had not started its advance. At Agua Nueva, the Arkansans faced a throng of problems. Horses were stolen and false alarms on impending attacks jangled their nerves. According to Samuel Chamberlain, a regular stationed nearby on that Christmas day, during a "stampede" to meet imagined Mexican troops, a group of volunteers—not necessarily Arkansans—raped some Mexican women. Alcohol available to the troops that day probably added to problems.[22] While on the march from San Antonio to Agua Nueva, General Wool had kept the volunteers under his command under fairly strict discipline. The events around Christmas were the beginning of a breakdown. Over the next few days, a portion of the Arkansas Regiment was moved to Patos. There some Arkansans traveling alone or in small groups were attacked, likely by rancheros in the region. At least one Arkansan believed that some of the troops had begun retaliating against Mexican civilians.[23] Attacks on all states' volunteers in the vicinity of Saltillo remained a concern, and likely raised the stress of the Arkansas troops.

Another event added to their anxiety. While on patrol around Encarnación—south of Agua Nueva—on Jan. 23, 1847, Maj. Solon Borland and about thirty-five Arkansans, along with a similar number of Kentucky volunteer cavalry, were taken prisoner. Because of particularly bad weather, a guard had been posted on top of the rancho where the troops were staying, but it was daylight before the Americans discovered that they were surrounded by lancers and other cavalry under Gen. J. V. Miñon, Santa Anna's scout to the north. When news of the capture reached Yell, he led a wild charge in the direction of Encarnacíon, evidently defying orders from his commanders to the contrary.[24] The Arkansas soldiers left at Agua Nueva were now shaken. An attack by Mexican forces seemed imminent. Gen. Zachary Taylor's troops in the area had been dramatically reduced by demands from Gen. Winfield Scott, and the Arkansans were still prey for highwaymen in the area.

The last straw came on Feb. 9, 1847, when Priv. Samuel H. Colquitt of Capt. C. C. Danley's company was ambushed and brutally killed while training a horse away from camp. After the body was found and buried, men from Danley's company and the Sevier County company went in search of those responsible for Colquitt's death.[25] The Arkansans, perhaps without their officers, searched the village of Catana and questioned Mexican civilians who reportedly possessed Colquitt's carbine sling and clothes belonging to a missing Illinois soldier. What happened next is not entirely clear. When the Arkansans didn't get the answers they sought from those living at the village, some of the Arkansas troops started shooting. Various reports from troops sent to investigate the gunshots suggest that between eighteen and thirty Mexicans were killed, some while begging for their lives.[26] Priv. Samuel Chamberlain's sometimes romantic memoirs have indicated that Arkansans engaged in scalping at a cave in the area during the massacre. While there are inconsistencies in Chamberlain's account and it is not clear that the unit of Dragoons of which he was a member were at the site, the assertion that some Mexican civilians were killed in a cave is reinforced by the fact Sgt. John C. Palmer's diary entry of Feb. 13 mentions the killings as having been in a cave and that seventeen were killed and more wounded.[27] This much is

Arkansas's reputation was bruised by the report of atrocities against Mexican civilians near Saltillo. The event was triggered by the ambush of a soldier in the Arkansas Regiment. (Painting by Sam Chamberlain from Sam Chamberlain's Mexican War, *courtesy of the San Jacinto Museum of History Paintings)*

not disputed: General Taylor was outraged by the killings and threatened both companies with being returned to the Rio Grande to face hard labor if the guilty parties were not identified to Taylor. But while the members of Danley's and Hunter's companies pondered this potential punishment, it became clear that Santa Anna's army was coming nearer and the men were needed to fight.[28] Ultimately, Taylor rescinded that order after General Wool came to the defense of the Arkansans, who he later argued had fought well in the battle of Buena Vista only days later.[29]

The Battles

The first hostile contact between Mexican and U.S. forces was that of Capt. Seth Thornton, who ran headlong into Gen. Anastasio Torrejón's forces above the Rio Grande in April 1846. There is no indication of Arkansans among those regulars, but there was seldom a time afterward when Arkansas troops, albeit often very few, were not involved in the fighting. Shortly after Thornton's skirmish, Gen. Zachary Taylor left Fort Texas—across the Rio Grande from Matamoros, Mexico—for Point Isabel to get supplies. On May 3, 1846, Mexican artillery at Matamoros began shelling the fort. On May 6, Maj. Jacob Brown of the Seventh Infantry, the commanding officer at the fort, was hit in the leg by a shell and wounded so seriously that his leg had to be amputated. While the fort was under siege, Taylor raced furiously back to supply it. In so doing he came face to face with Gen. Mariano Arista's troops, first in the battle of Palo Alto, then the next day at the battle of Resaca de la Palma. Back at Fort Texas, although clearly in excruciating pain, Brown remained calm. As the surgeons began to take care of Brown, the major noticed that some of his men were lingering too long at his bedside while the shelling of the fort continued. He told

Maj. Jacob Brown was among the first casualties along the Rio Grande. The death of this former Arkansas resident helped spark enlistment in the state. (From John Frost, Pictorial History of Mexico and the Mexican War, 1853, *courtesy of Bill Frazier)*

them, "Men, go to your duties, stand by your posts; I am but one among you." As Taylor's army was winning the battle, Major Brown passed away in the stifling heat of a "bomb proof" on May 9—Arkansas's first casualty of the war.[30]

Jacob Brown fits the profile of a man who Arkansans viewed as one of their own. The 58-year-old major was originally from Massachusetts but had lived in Arkansas some years in the 1830s while working as a disbursing officer for the Indian Office in the War Department. Without surrendering his commission, Brown was named president of the Arkansas State Bank. He had been well connected with U.S. Senator Chester Ashley and was well known to the people of Little Rock: they called him a townsman.[31] A few days after Brown's death, General Taylor had paid him respect by changing the name of Fort Texas to Fort Brown.[32]

Those events did not go unnoticed in Arkansas. When news of Brown's death reached the state, it helped fuel a flurry of recruiting activity for the Arkansas Mounted Gunmen bound for Mexico and the infantry battalion destined for the Indian Territory. Brown's death helped give life to the first units of Arkansas soldiers to fight in a war. Granted, some Arkansans were involved as state troops during the Indian wars. But this war was expected to be history writ large. There was glory to be had; an Arkansan already had a fort named in his honor.

There had been another Arkansas soldier at Fort Texas, a Brevet 2nd Lt. Erastus B. Strong in the Seventh Infantry. Strong was transferred to the Fifth Infantry after the actions along the Rio Grande, and might well have been the only Arkansan to fight in the battle of Monterrey in September 1846.[33]

The next battle, Buena Vista, involved more Arkansas soldiers than any other. In late February 1847, only 479 of the original regiment of 870 were available to take part in the battle of Buena Vista. Still, this was the largest number of Arkansans in any battle in the war.[34] For this reason, Buena Vista deserves particular attention. First, a quick look at the order of battle shows that Arkansans composed about ten percent of Taylor's force.[35]

Cavalry

Arkansas Mounted Gunmen (Col. Archibald Yell)	**479**
1st Kentucky Cavalry (Col. Humphrey Marshall)	305
1st Dragoons (Capt. Enoch Steen)	133
2nd Dragoons (Lt. Col. Charles May)	76
Texas Rangers (unknown)	61
Texas Spy Company (Maj. Ben McCulloch)	27

Infantry

1st Illinois (Col. John J. Hardin)	580
2nd Illinois (Col. William H. Bissell)	573
2nd Kentucky (Col. William R. McKee)	571
Indiana Brigade (Brig. Gen. Joseph Lane)	1,253
2nd Indiana (Col. William A. Bowles)	
3rd Indiana (Col. James H. Lane)	
1st Mississippi Rifles (Col. Jefferson Davis)	368

Artillery

Battery, 4th Artillery (Capt. J. M. Washington)	117
Battery, 3rd Artillery (Capt. Braxton Bragg)	150
Battery, 3rd Artillery (Capt. Thomas W. Sherman)	150
General Staff (Gens. Zachary Taylor/John E. Wool)	41

Total U.S forces	**4,750**

This battle is difficult to visualize because of the geography and time that it covers. Many of the Arkansans involved had little rest from the night of Feb. 21 through the night of Feb. 23 and some through the next day. An examination of the numbers available for duty in the Arkansas Regiment, 479, gives some indication of the number of men who had suffered from illness and death along the way. But that number does not reflect how the troops were allocated. First, a full squadron—something less than one hundred men under Captains Albert Pike (Pulaski County) and John Preston (Phillips County)—was detailed to ride with the Second Dragoons under Lt. Col. Charles May. Thus Yell's command likely had less than four hundred men.

Yell's men had been stationed at Agua Nueva off and on since December 1846. Sightings of Santa Anna's army near the rancho Encarnacíon in February had given Taylor reason to believe he was soon to be attacked. He sent word to Agua Nueva to begin moving supplies out of that forward position on Feb. 21, but not to allow those supplies to be captured. Yell's Arkansans were assigned the duty of guarding the teamsters as they loaded supplies at the rancho. When pickets south of Buena Vista were heard shooting on the night of Feb. 21, there was chaos among the poorly disciplined Arkansas troops. Assuming that the enemy was only minutes away, some panicked teamsters allowed wagons to become hopelessly entangled. Horses were spooked and ran away before being hitched, forcing several wagons to be abandoned. The rancho with its remaining stores and a large stack of wheat were set afire. Jonathon H. Buhoup, a sergeant in Danley's Pulaski County company, said that the Arkansans formed up in front of the rancho but out of the light of the fire and waited some two hours to see if they could open a volley on the Mexicans before leaving, but left before Santa Anna's troops arrived.[36] Buhoup didn't leave us nearly as poetic an account of the event as did James Henry Carleton, one of Gen. Wool's aides:

The burning of the buildings, and of several large stacks of unthreshed grain, illumined [sic] the whole valley of La Encantada, and painted the rugged and picturesque features of the surrounding mountains in bright relief against the murky shadows of the intervening gorges. Perhaps no single picture of some of the most striking effects of the war could produce a stronger or more lasting impression, than the one here exhibited. The noise of the falling timbers, the roar of the flames, the huge column of ascending smoke, the appearance of armed and mounted men moving between the spectator and the fire, with brilliant light flashing here and there on burnished arms and glittering appointments,—taken in connection with scattered shots interchanged between still other of our advanced parties and those of Ampudia, the heavy rumbling of our rapidly retreating train of wagons, intermingled with the distant trumpet ... now and then faintly heard in the distance of the approaching enemy,— all conspired to render that cold, deep midnight one that could never be forgotten.[37]

The Arkansans were told to march in good order back toward the main army, but good order never being their strong suit, they went on a tear. They reached the southern end of the valley where Col. William R. McKee's men escorted them in, finally reaching Buena Vista about 4 a.m., where they bedded down quickly and tried to get some rest. It was to be their first of several anxious nights.[38]

It is not clear who was responsible for picking the defensive position that the Americans had chosen, although General Wool often gets credit. The battlefield we call Buena Vista, for a rancho at the northern end, was called by the Mexicans of the region La Angostura, or the Narrows. It is a long gap in the Sierra Madre mountains on the best road between San Luis Potosí and Saltillo. As the road comes through La Angostura, it is flanked on the west

This cathedral in Saltillo was used as a hospital after the battle of Buena Vista. (Courtesy of the Yale Collection of Western Americana, Beinecke Rare Book and Manuscript Library)

by deep gullies that are almost impassable. On the east was fairly level ground, but raised as much as 40 feet above the road and backed to the east by steep mountains. It was on this broad, elevated plain cut with gullies by years of erosion that the Americans made their defense of the road, allowing them fairly easy movement of their artillery and cavalry. The Mexican army, by contrast, was forced to either fight its way up the road under a withering fire from artillery and infantry or fight a literally uphill battle against Taylor's troops on the plain.

Santa Anna's troops had been stretched out in their long march from Encarnacíon to Agua Nueva, and when the first of Santa Anna's men arrived at Agua Nueva in the early morning hours of Feb. 22, the fires of the burning supplies convinced the Mexican commander that the Americans were in retreat. Rather than allowing his men time to rest at Agua Nueva, he pressed them forward, with little opportunity for food after a miserable march with little water.[39]

On the morning of Feb. 22, the Arkansas Regiment minus Pike's squadron—something less than four hundred men—were split into two commands. Those armed with rifles were to be used dismounted under Lt. Col. John Seldon Roane. The remainder, mounted and under the command of Colonel Yell, were stationed with the Kentucky cavalry along the American left at the base of the mountains. Pike's squadron saw no battle on Feb. 22, spending much of the day defending Saltillo. At about 8 a.m., Pike's men were part of the group that escorted

John Seldon Roane was Speaker of the House in the Arkansas legislature before the war and elected lieutenant colonel in the Arkansas Regiment. (Courtesy of the Arkansas History Commission)

General Taylor to the battlefield, then it was back to Saltillo's rooftops to wait. General Miñon's cavalry threatened but did not attack the city throughout the battle. Recalled John C. Palmer, a 22-year-old sergeant of the Phillips County company:

Gen. Minon is now in sight of the town with his cavalry, say 3000. They stayed at Palomas last night and [may] have reached there a few hours after we left. They keep maneuvering, but do not approach. The cannonading at "Buena Vista" still continues. ... The night is to be passed by us in a state of watchfulness, and our horses are to remain saddled. I sleep on top of the houses, ready, booted and spurred."[40]

It was about 9 a.m. that the enemy came in sight, and an alarm sounded. The First Illinois had erected a parapet of sorts furthest to the south, and were standing atop it cheering as the Mexican army came into view, perhaps surprising the Mexicans who might have been expecting a full retreat to Saltillo.[41]

Santa Anna had lost a significant portion of his army in his march from San Luis Potosí; at least four thousand had become ill, deserted or died en route. Still he was in charge of more than fifteen thousand men, as compared to 4,750 under Taylor.[42] It took some hours for the Mexican army to file into the valley, as the road was narrow and the ground was rough. As this was happening, Wool stirred the fire in his men, reminding them that it was Washington's birthday and they should do nothing to dishonor his memory. He was met company by company with cheers of "The Memory of Washington!"[43] At about 11 a.m., Taylor rode from Saltillo to the battlefield, bringing loud cheers again from the Americans and about this time, Taylor received from Santa Anna, under a white flag, an invitation to surrender:

You are surrounded by twenty thousand men, and cannot in any human possibility avoid suffering a rout and being cut to pieces with your troops; but as you deserve consideration and particular esteem, I wish to save you from catastrophe, and for that purpose give you this notice in order that you may surrender at discretion, under the assurance that you will be treated with consideration belonging to the Mexican character. ... God and Liberty!

The exact words under which Taylor declined are not written for posterity, but have been suggested to be profane. The written answer was somewhat more formal:

In reply to your note of this date, summoning me to surrender my forces at your discretion, I beg leave to say that I decline acceding to your request.[44]

It was almost 2 p.m. before Santa Anna had enough troops in the valley to begin the battle. General Ampudia's men moved to the left and began scaling the left with hopes of flanking the Americans from the high ground. Taylor ordered Col. Humphrey Marshall to take part of his Kentucky cavalry, Roane's Arkansas riflemen and part of the Indiana Infantry up an opposing ridge to meet the threat.[45] Over time, artillery pieces under Lt. John Paul Jones O'Brien and more Illinois and Indiana infantry would move to support them along their right flank. The first shots of the battle seem to have been fired along the road. But a short time afterward, the artillery opened, and the Arkansans and Mexicans exchanged small arms fire across a long hollow. Priv. William Quesenbury of Fayetteville, who was evidently with Yell's men below, recalled in a letter how the battle opened:

Our army, at the first approach of the enemy, had been formed upon the field, but we rested upon our arms till 3 o'clock, P.M., when the enemy fired a gun—a nine-pounder, I think it was. Did you ever hear the first gun of battle? It breaks the expectancy, and speaks that the die will soon be cast. At the sound we started to our feet; but some time passed before we heard another, and we were soon lolling on the ground, joking about the coming events. ... There is a large mountain on the left of the battle field, looking towards the south; and it was on the side of this mountain that we first discovered the Mexicans. At the distance of two miles, they could be plainly seen marching up the steeps by thousands, and all so regular that they looked like a vast black belt that girded the eminences.[46]

The Mexicans kept up a steady barrage against the American forces, but they were hampered by weaker powder combined with the use of muskets. The American troops, many of them using rifles, picked their shots from behind cover with more effect. But the most serious of the fighting that day lasted only about an hour. The time of the year and the height of the mountains led to an early evening at La Angostura. Mexican commanders fired a rocket as a signal to stop the attack as night fell and generally the only shots exchanged overnight came from nervous pickets on the edges of the battlefield. One of Wool's officers reported later that the American casualties that day were perhaps only four wounded. But the deadly accuracy of the American rifles had led to almost three hundred among the Mexican forces.[47]

As dark came, Santa Anna gave another speech to his troops. The Arkansans, trying to rest, could not have heard his words. But from down the valley, like other troops, they likely heard the response of Santa Anna's men: "Viva Santana! Viva Republica! Libertad o Muerte!"[48]

As the Arkansas soldiers tried to get some rest, another drama for some Arkansans came to an end. A Lieutenant Tomberlin—either Thomas C. Tomberlin or John W. Tomberlin, both of Preston's Company—rode in with his picket of some 20 men. As the pickets had been driven in the night before near Aqua Nueva, an express rider had been sent to call in Tomberlin and his men. The now unknown express rider never reached Tomberlin; in fact, he never returned, perhaps being killed or captured by Santa Anna's advancing troops. Tomberlin's pickets spent the night at rancho San Juan watching flames glimmer along the mountains. Assuming it was a grass fire, a not uncommon occurrence, they worried little about the fires at Agua Nueva. About 10 a.m. on Feb. 22, when no one came to his relief, Tomberlin took his men back toward Agua Nueva. Near there he saw what he believed was a troop of Dragoons and started toward them. The men he guessed were Dragoons were Mexican cavalrymen, who likewise thought that the Arkansans were their own troops. The two groups figured out their mistake at about the same time and the race was on. The Arkansas men were outnumbered, but had one advantage: bigger, faster horses. Over the course of the day, the Mexicans and Tomberlin's men played a cat-and-mouse game through the mountains. When it became clear to Tomberlin that his horses could outrun the Mexicans' mounts, he even taunted the opposing cavalry; his men gave three cheers to Mexicans on a nearby ridge and beckoned the Mexicans onward. But the Mexican cavalry must have feared a trap, for their troops broke off and left the Americans to sneak back to safety. This in itself was a hazardous task; in the dark, one group of soldiers does not look much different from another at a safe distance. The Arkansans eventually worked their way around the mountains and ran into the Americans between Saltillo and Buena Vista at 10 p.m., rejoining the Arkansas troops that night. It was a relief to Yell, who believed they were all dead or prisoners.[49]

Settling in on the night of Feb. 22, most of the Arkansans and the other Americans along the ridge were called back down to the men on the plateau. Some, however, spent a fitful night along the side of the mountain where a cold rain made sleep difficult. The men gathered weeds and yucca plants to make fires—the only fires among the Americans on the battlefield. By 2 a.m., there were a few gunshots, for the Mexicans were on the move up the mountain, again flanking the Americans.[50]

On the morning of Feb. 23, 1847, four companies of Arkansas
soldiers and a squadron of Kentucky cavalry were sent to the left
"somewhat in the rear of the Second Indiana Regiment under Col.
William Bowles, and Lieut. O'Brien's section of Artillery,"
Sergeant Buhoup said. The remainder, evidently still under
Roane's command, rejoined their compatriots on the mountain. At
about the same time that an attack was launched on the First
Illinois Infantry near the road, the Mexican forces along the
mountain opened up on the Arkansans there. A series of events led
to the panic for which the Arkansas troops became known.
Sergeant Buhoup describes it thus:

> The whole of this time the four companies of Arkansas
> Cavalry, were under a most galling fire from the infantry
> in the front, and a cross fire of grape and canister from
> the battery posted on our left, without having orders to
> return the compliment. O'Brien returned fire with his
> guns, as did the 2d Indiana Regiment, but by some
> mistake Col Bowls [sic] gave the unfortunate orders to
> cease firing and retreat, which they did in great disorder.
> On running over the ravine, they came across the horses
> belonging to the Arkansas and Kentucky riflemen, who
> were dismounted and in the mountain. Some of these
> they mounted, and pushed off for safer quarters. This was
> what gave rise to the report of the Arkansas Regiment
> having retreated, as the men appeared like Arkansas men,
> being mounted on their horses. Any one at a distance
> would have been led to believe they were such. ... About
> this time, Colonels Yell and Marshall, discovering that
> the enemy was attempting to cut off the riflemen, who
> were in imminent danger, gained an advantageous plat of
> ground, and charged the enemy's lines with intrepidity
> and courage. Here for the first time the enemy was driven
> back. By this advantage over the enemy, the riflemen
> were enabled to escape from the impending danger. Some

got their horses and joined their regiment, and those who had no horses went on to the rancho.[51]

It's safe to assume that there is some truth to Sergeant Buhoup's account. Perhaps in the panic that followed the Second Indiana's fleeing the field, some did gather up Arkansans' horses. But some of the Arkansas soldiers took off, too, with some halting at the rancho Buena Vista. Others ran all the way to Saltillo and claimed all was lost. It was one of two low points for Arkansas troops in the battle. To their credit, some Arkansans did attempt to stop the flanking maneuver of the Mexican army along the American left. Said Josiah Gregg, who was traveling with the Arkansas men, "the volunteer cavalry should not be left to fight on horseback. Their horses are useful for scouting, pursuits, etc. but when brought into regular battle they should be dismounted. Neither their horses nor themselves are trained—they are 'out of their elements'—can neither shoot nor use their sabers; but put them on foot, the way they have been in the habit of shooting, and they are very efficient soldiers." Charles May's Dragoons and Pike's men were called for support along the left.[52]

The American position at 9 a.m. that morning was troubling. Santa Anna's army had turned the American left, dispersed a regiment of Indiana infantry and the Arkansas and Kentucky cavalry, captured two of O'Brien's artillery pieces, and gained a toe-hold on the plateau, the last place Taylor wanted Mexican forces. Santa Anna tried desperately to take advantage of the latter, sending a division of troops led by cavalry further along the left as it tried to take three sides of the American position. The Mississippi Rifles, under Jefferson Davis, and the Third Indiana Infantry, perhaps with a smattering of those who had fled the earlier battles, met the attacking Mexicans in an inverted "V" position. As the Mexican cavalry closed within seventy yards, the

Americans fired simultaneously and the Mississippians finished off many dazed Mexicans with Bowie knives.[53]

There was hard fighting on the massive battlefield that day, but the most significant with regard to the Arkansans came later. Colonels Yell and Marshall noticed U.S. supply wagons moving toward the rancho Buena Vista, perhaps to be pointed toward Saltillo if a full retreat was called. The two colonels also observed that a body of Mexican cavalry had also spied the wagons, and was making for them. The remnants of the two American mounted regiments were now at a strength of between 350 and 450 men. The two colonels determined to make a charge and halt the Mexicans. Private Quesenbury's account of the action may be the clearest:

> The lancers, about two thousand strong, bore down upon us; at a distance of about 100 yards we fired upon them. They sprung at the fire and we charged them. They separated in two divisions, one on our left and the other on our right. We pressed those on the left and the work of death was raging. If balls and lances, sabers, smoke and dust, shouting, groaning, an dying compose glory, we were in the midst of it. Not a word was spoken—it was all fighting. ... The Mexicans tumbled on every side. I saw them struck down with sabres and trampled to death beneath our horses' feet. I saw them beg with uplifted hands for mercy, it was remembered that those very hands had driven lances into the very hearts of our countrymen.[54]

In the process of the short skirmish, Yell's horse had bolted well ahead of the remainder of his troops. The cause for this is not perfectly clear; Buhoup indicated that the bit in Yell's horse's mouth broke and that he could not control his mount. In any event, he was felled by multiple lance wounds, including one to the head.[55] Capt. Andrew Porter of Independence County was killed when his head was split by a saber. Another Arkansan whose death got more

Colonel Archibald Yell was killed Feb. 23, 1847, during a charge against Mexican lancers at Buena Vista. His body was among the few to be disinterred and returned to Arkansas for reburial. (From John Frost, Pictorial History of Mexico and the Mexican War, 1853, *courtesy of Bill Frazier)*

than a little attention was John Pelham, a Little Rock boy of a prominent family, who died of multiple lance wounds after being dislodged from his horse.[56]

As the Mexican cavalry split, some veered back toward the mountains from whence they had come; others ripped through the road at the rancho Buena Vista. There some officers had placed on the rooftops perhaps as many as two hundred soldiers displaced from their units earlier in the day, some likely Arkansans, and those Americans kept the Mexican cavalry moving with a continuous fire. The effect of the charge, the arrival of May and Pike, and the barrage at the rancho served to end the threat on the extremes of the American left.[57]

There was more fighting that day, but none quite so serious for the Arkansas troops. It is almost impossible to discern what portion of the Arkansans fled the battlefield, but some certainly did. Some never left. Over the span of the next several days, at least fifteen Arkansas men were buried in the hollows at the base of the mountains at La Angostura. The Arkansans suffered forty-two casualties—eighteen killed, twenty-three wounded and one missing.[58] The Arkansas troops also lost some company flags. By one account, those captured included one that read "Extend the Area of Freedom," which belonged to Danley's company. The other "Rackensack, is in the Field," although unclear to which company it belonged, was clearly another Arkansas flag.[59] In the days that followed, the Arkansans had time to reflect on their actions in the state's first major battle. Said Private Quesenbury of the flight of the Arkansas troops, "When they heard the tide had turned, they came back (the most of them) and were loud in their accounts of their own valor. Men fled to Saltillo that we thought were brave; and men fought that we thought were wavering."[60]

The night of Feb. 23 was no less anxious for the Arkansas men than were the previous two. Fires at Santa Anna's camps burned bright, but with the morning it became clear that his men had left the field. They were in fact starting the long march toward Mexico City. Santa Anna had ever committed enough of his troops to win the battle the Americans came to call Buena Vista, and Taylor's men had held on. When the sun came up the next morning there were long cheers from the Americans. For the Arkansas soldiers, half starved from eating little but raw bacon, there was one saving grace—a herd of sheep came into the valley and were descended upon by the men. Buhoup said "not one remained or escaped."[61]

Over the next several days, the wounded and ill were cared for in makeshift hospitals, including the cathedral at Saltillo and the rancho Buena Vista. According to one account, the use of pasteboard splints took care of many of the breaks, and there were relatively few amputations. Those who died in those places were buried nearby.[62] In the case of Yell, Porter and Pelham, they were

Gen. Zachary Taylor was in command of Arkansas Troops at the Battle of Buena Vista in 1847. Combined with earlier victories along the Rio Grande and at Monterrey, it helped him be elected president in 1848. (Courtesy of the Library of Congress Prints and Photographs Division)

specifically buried at sites where the bodies would not be disturbed and they could be disinterred later. Yell's body was placed inside a tin coffin, then that was placed inside a stronger wooden coffin and buried within sight of Capt. L. B. Webster's "fort," just south of Saltillo. Others buried nearby were Col. John J. Hardin of the First Illinois Infantry and Capt. George Lincoln, the adjutant general on Wool's staff.[63] Taylor sent dragoons and some of the Arkansans to Agua Nueva, then to Encarnacíon, to discuss the exchange of prisoners—the Americans had some three hundred—and take provisions to the desperate Mexicans left behind there. The U.S. forces were specifically looking to negotiate the release of the Encarnacíon prisoners, and it was agreed to by both sides, but did not happen.[64]

The remainder of the Arkansans' stay near the Buena Vista battlefield was not without incident, but for the Regiment of Mounted Gunmen, the most significant fighting was finished. Mostly they bided their time and waited to go home as the Mexican army and the war with the Americans shifted to the south.

Mexico City campaign

As the winter of 1846-47 brought to Arkansas news of the troops' miserable conditions—disease, death and desertion—the Twelfth Infantry was recruiting in the state. There had been fervor to join only months before, but the realities of war had discouraged recruiting for the companies of Captains Wood and Banks. Still, Wood's company was almost entirely recruited in Arkansas, and in early 1847 was went downriver to New Orleans to finish training for the next phase of the war— Gen. Winfield Scott's invasion of Vera Cruz and march to Mexico City.

At the Vera Cruz landing in March 1847, Gen. William Worth's division was the first to slog ashore. Among the units under Worth's command was the Fifth Infantry, and with it Lt. Erastus Strong of Arkansas.[65] Also coming ashore that day was Capt. Stephen S. Tucker, a Little Rock man of

Gen. Winfield Scott led the U.S. invasion of central Mexico starting at Vera Cruz. His occupation of Mexico City in September 1847 eventually led to Mexico's capitulation. (Courtesy of the Library of Congress Prints and Photographs Division)

the U.S. Regiment of Mounted Rifles, who were U.S. Army regulars. The landing and siege of Vera Cruz were proud moments for the Americans; the casualties were almost nonexistent. But the Mounted Rifles suffered somewhat: the regiment lost the majority of its horses in transport across the gulf and was afoot for most of the fighting in Mexico.[66]

Tucker was certainly involved in the battle that followed, Cerro Gordo, but may have been the only Arkansan that fought there. His account of Cerro Gordo is not the clearest from the war, but is among the most colorful. The uphill fight on the mountain El Telegrafo he sums up thus:

> Infantry, artillery, volunteers and rifles, simultaneously! Merciful God!—such another shower of metal,—iron, lead and copper. The shouting of the Americans, the din of the artillery, the keen crack of the Rifles, the spang of the musket, and bumble-bee buzz of the d—d escopet, made old mother earth groan as we stamped and raved over her rocky breast.[67]

When the Twelfth Infantry landed at Vera Cruz in July 1847, it was immediately ordered to join Scott's army inland to replace volunteers whose term of enlistment had expired. Under the command of Gen. Franklin Pierce the march toward Puebla was eventful; the Twelfth—and thus the Arkansans in two companies there—was involved in at least five skirmishes with Mexican troops, the most notable at the National Bridge, not far from El Telegrafo.[68] The Twelfth joined Scott's army at Puebla in August, but without their colonel, Louis D. Wilson, who was assigned to other duties before his death at Vera Cruz. Command devolved to Lt. Col. Milledge L. Bonham. Capt. Allen Wood, a Carroll County man, was in charge of two companies on the march from Vera Cruz. With Pierce's men at Puebla, Winfield Scott's army grew to 10,738 men—not as many as he had wanted, but enough to start his march on the Valley of Mexico. Most of that trip across the mountains was uneventful, but Santa Anna had been given plenty of time to prepare to defend Mexico City. Scott's decision to bypass Santa Anna's largest forces on the eastern edge of the city allowed the Americans to use the lakes as a shield as they flanked Santa Anna to the south. In so doing, one of his engineers, the indefatigable Capt. Robert E. Lee, was forced to find a way around a natural feature that was almost impassable, the four-mile wide lava field known as El Pedregal. Lee discovered that a road could be cut through a small portion of the lava field, and in so doing it allowed U.S. troops to secretly prepare themselves for an attack on Gen. Gabriel Valencia, who had disregarded Santa Anna's orders and stationed his men beyond the support of the main body of the Mexican army. As U.S. artillery bounced along jagged lava roads with young Lieutenants George B. McClellan and Thomas J. (later Stonewall) Jackson giving orders, the Twelfth Infantry made its way through the edge of the lava field. When Valencia's men told their commander that Americans were coming through the Pedregal, he dismissed them, saying "No! No! You're dreaming young man. The birds couldn't cross the Pedregal."[69]

Sending Pierce's brigade, now minus its wounded general, was an afterthought by Scott on the night of Aug.19; he was trying to reinforce troops he was nervous might already be overextended. As Capt. John Magruder's artillery kept Valencia looking southward, the road across the Pedragal allowed the Americans to sneak into position and, in the case of Wood's men, out of position as well. Over the span of a half a day, Wood's men crossed the Pedregal coming and going three times. In the process several men were mildly injured, including Wood, who suffered a nasty contusion but kept command. Bonham, however, was injured, and command of perhaps all of the Twelfth Infantry, but at least a battalion, devolved to Captain Wood. When the Ninth and Twelfth Infantries made a feint on Valencia's front that morning, the Mexicans were hit from the rear by other American forces. Valencia's troops, cut off from reinforcement by Santa Anna, were dispersed in seventeen minutes at what came to be called the battle of Contreras. Said Wood of the fighting, "We all hastened as rapidly as the ground would permit, forded the stream, and poured into their dismayed ranks a most destructive fire."[70] The shock of the American troops sent Valencia and his men fleeing, with Valencia dodging the wrath of Santa Anna as much as the Americans.

Contreras and Churubusco are separated by very little time or geography and it is debatable if they can be called two separate battles as much as one continuous moving fight. As the Americans pursued Valencia's men north, the Arkansans were ordered to take positions on the western flank of Santa Anna's forces at Churubusco. Crossing the Churubusco River well west of the worst fighting that had erupted to the east, Wood's men were ordered into a position that would harass Santa Anna's rear and retreat, if and when it happened, toward Mexico City. Using the opportunity of the fight to come out of hiding was Maj. Solon Borland, a prisoner of Encarnacíon. He ran headlong into Capt. Stephen Tucker and, after a warm embrace, ended up shouldering a musket for much of the day's fighting. Wood's men spent much of the midday firing at the Tulancingo Cuirassiers (cavalry), the Eleventh Line and the Mexican Fourth Light Regiment. Wood later said of the attack:[71]

> I directed my advance to a wa[l]l about three feet high, situated on their right flank, behind which I placed my men who opened a rapid and destructive fire upon them, while we were so well protected they could make no compensating impression upon our ran[k]s. More than two hours did this terrific conflict continue, but the enemy finally wavered, fell back, and the day was ours.[72]

In the fighting that day, the Americans captured a significant amount of Mexican artillery. Recaptured were the two pieces that Lieutenant O'Brien had lost at the battle of Buena Vista as the American left disintegrated on Feb. 23.

The men of the Twelfth Infantry were effectively out of the fight for the remainder of combat around Mexico City, being relegated to guarding prisoners and the artillery park. But Lieutenant Strong of St. Francis County was among those on the horrific list of casualties at Molino del Rey. Two more Arkansans—Maj. Solon Borland and Capt. C.C. Danley—served notably in the battle for Chapultepec and later in the fighting to the gates of Mexico City, both being used to carry dispatches on the field.[73]

An Arkansan figured in the peace, as well. Senator Ambrose Sevier, as head of the foreign relations committee, shepherded the Treaty of Guadalupe Hidalgo through the U.S. Senate and later was part of the commission to see that it was ratified in Mexico. It was Sevier who packed the treaty into his saddlebags for the ride home after it had been ratified in the Mexican Congress in 1848.[74]

American newspapers recounted the atrocities of the Arkansas troops near Agua Nueva, and accounts of the fleeing Arkansans at Buena Vista colored the nation's view of the state's troops. Arkansas had lost battle flags, an embarrassment for the state, and they were not recaptured in the U.S. occupation of Mexico City. That may seem an unlikely circumstance, but was not implausible since Lieutenant O'Brien's artillery pieces were recaptured near Mexico City. Even now, the engraving on the two pieces, which are housed at the U.S. Military Academy's

U.S. Senator Ambrose Sevier of Arkansas spearheaded President James K. Polk's treaty with Mexico, then packed the treaty into his saddlebags for the ride home after it had been ratified by the Mexican Congress in 1848. (Courtesy of the Arkansas History Commission)

Building 600, reflect the army's pride in its artillerymen: "Lost without Dishonor: Recovered with Glory." From a national view, Arkansas's successes at the same battles where those guns were recaptured, Contreras and Churubusco, could not recover Arkansas's lost honor or, in the broad sense, cover its troops with glory.

It is difficult to assess how Arkansans viewed their troops' first war experiences. Their reflections were forever marked by the fact that some fled at Buena Vista, a stark contrast to the heroic actions of Jefferson Davis's Mississippians. It caused embarrassment within the community and helped fuel the Roane-Pike duel after the Arkansans arrived home. On July 18, 1847, as the steamer *Hatchee Planter* pulled in at Little Rock, carrying the body of Archibald Yell, troops from the Arkansas Regiment poured out to a rousing reception. The father of Sgt. John D. Adams said to his son, "I'm told you fought like h—l at Buena Vista." The young son replied wryly, "We ran like h—l at Buena Vista."[75] It came to be the prevailing view of Arkansas's embarrassment from the war. But a significant number of Arkansans acted honorably and fought bravely in the war and thus the soldiers, if not the public, likely saw the less-than-heroic actions as anomalies. So it should come as no surprise that more than one Arkansan wrote home of how well they had performed—certainly that was the case with Wood, writing after the battles into the Valley of Mexico. Even after Buena Vista there was some pride. The troops knew they had wavered, but still they had survived their first trial under fire. That sense of success for many may be best summed up briefly by a line in a letter home from Lt. Davis Thompson of Phillips County: "The fight on the 23d lasted for ten hours—sometimes I thought they had us; but I am now perfectly satisfied all h—l can't whip us."[76]

The View from the Other Side: Mexican Historiographical Perspectives on the 1846-1848 War With the United States

By Pedro Santoni

In 1995, as a nameless young New Jersey high school teacher started his daily 30-minute commute to school and looked ahead to his classes, he thought about a daunting predicament that lay ahead: "to dream of new ways of lifting the monumentally forgettable Mexican War off the textbook page and into his students' imagination."[1] Several factors help explain the lack of public interest in an event "of major importance" to the development of the United States as a nation; they include the fact that the war with Mexico was neither a massive affair nor a total victory, that the U.S. Civil War overshadowed the 1846-1848 conflict in the popular imagination, and the widely perceived notion of the conflict with the United States' southern neighbor as unjust.[2] Such amnesia in the U.S. consciousness remains extant. Early in January 2004 a correspondent for *The New York Times* pointed out that "almost no one [in the U.S.] remembers the war that Americans fought against Mexico more than 150 years ago." In Mexico, on the other hand, few have "forgotten [the confrontation]." Not only did the armed struggle between the adjoining countries deprive Mexico of half its territory, but it also left—in the words of historian Miguel Soto—a "wound [that] never really healed."[3] The abrasion has since manifested itself in a "virulent, almost pathological, Yankeephobia" that drives Mexican nationalism and surfaces in a variety of settings.[4] It emerges during periods of domestic crisis, leaves its mark on issues that affect bilateral relations like immigration, water resources, and the war on drugs, and materializes on the soccer field as well, where the U.S. and Mexico compete in "the most heated international rivalry in North American sports."[5]

Given that reverberations from an event as powerful as the U.S.-Mexican War remain deeply embedded in the Mexican psyche, this essay—in keeping with the goals of the seminar held at the Old State House Museum—provides a historiographical analysis of Mexican viewpoints about the conflict. It first focuses on the four "most representative" first-hand Mexican interpretations of the conflict, those of Mariano Otero, José Fernando Ramírez, Carlos María Bustamante, and the fifteen-member team headed by Ramón Alcaraz.[6] These authors, like most nineteenth-century Mexican writers, were "self-educated, multifaceted people who worked in many professions—as journalists, educators, administrators, clerics, politicians, and lawyers. All wrote history as an avocation [and] ... were intensely political,"[7] but they also possessed a sharp eye for the contours of Mexican society. After analyzing how Otero, Ramírez, Bustamante, and Alcaraz explained Mexico's failure to respond to the challenge of self-defense, the essay then considers how subsequent accounts on the war have validated and/or modified their insights. Finally, this article looks at a number of recent scholarly endeavors that have enhanced public understanding of the war by examining heretofore neglected areas of the conflict. Such efforts will hopefully spark popular interest in the war and ensure that it finally receives the attention it deserves.

★★★

In the aftermath of a bitter eleven-year struggle that led to emancipation from Spain in 1821, many public-spirited Mexicans looked to the future with unbridled optimism. They believed that emulating the U.S. could ensure "national greatness" for the new nation. Some individuals, however, remained skeptical. Creole priest Servando Teresa de Mier, a staunch supporter of Mexican independence who also helped design the 1824 Mexican federal constitution, realized that "institutions alone could not explain American success,"[8] and his caveat became a reality during the next two decades. The former strong and stable Viceroyalty of New Spain turned into a republic that suffered from economic decline, political and social turmoil, and class hatreds on the eve of war with the U.S. This chaotic state of affairs did not restrain the rhetoric of the vibrant Mexico City press at such a crucial time. Determined to preserve their country's honor and its territorial integrity after the U.S. had annexed Texas in late February 1845, several Mexican newspapers helped fuel an ill-begotten sense of bravado that pressured government authorities to pursue a belligerent policy toward their northern neighbor. Such hollow blustering was no longer evident as 1847 came to an end. By that time U.S. armies not only held much of northern Mexico, but they also had marched east from Vera Cruz and occupied the national capital. Mexico's failure to effectively meet the U.S. threat fostered a sense of profound despair that prompted Mexican pundits to look for explanations for the military defeat and obtain a better understanding of the ailments that had immobilized the country.

The first of these works to appear in print was *Consideraciones sobre la situación política y social de la república mexicana en el año de 1847*. Published early in 1848 and probably authored by Mariano Otero, a professional politician who had first made his mark in public affairs in the early 1840s, the pamphlet offered an unflattering portrayal of Mexican society at mid-century.[9] In the first of its two parts Otero surveyed the make-up of the Mexican population as well as the driving forces behind the economy, and found little to praise in each. Almost four million of Mexico's approximate seven million inhabitants were Indians who remained, as he put it, in a "sorrowful existence." Of the remaining three million white and mixed-blood inhabitants, nearly two-thirds were "women, children, and old people." That left 1.2 million men as "potentially useful," but only the three hundred thousand men employed in agriculture, manufacturing, mining, and commerce fit into this category; the remainder he labeled as "unproductive classes." Such an acute imbalance, according to Otero, led to "the impoverishment and stagnation of all the sources of public wealth" and undermined the "most flourishing nation on earth." He found commerce to be "languishing," farmlands in a "general state of neglect," the administration of justice "in chaos," manufacturing in decline, and artisans "ineffective and despised." Only mining offered a glimmer of hope because it gave "indication of increasing prosperity," but the spark was dim because the industry's profits went to the mine owners and those "engaged in their exploitation."[10]

Otero took to task two of the most important and powerful institutions in early republican Mexico—the military and the Church—as well as the bureaucracy in the second part of *Consideraciones*. His scrutiny of both influential establishments was likewise uncomplimentary. Otero found the army to have "undoubtedly [been] the most immediately responsible for our loss of national honor." He characterized most officers as "ignorant and corrupt men," and chastised the government for not providing the few capable ones with inducements to fulfill their duties. Meanwhile, not only did Otero hold the clergy largely accountable for "all the misfortunes of the nation," but he also censured them (as this essay later shows) for having shown a "cold selfishness" in the struggle with the U.S. that he attributed to the "ignorance of its members" and the "inequality of wealth" among them. Finally, Otero asserted that most government officials were noted for their "scandalous corruption and ineptitude." In the end, these considerations led Otero to ask why Mexicans had failed to rise up in defense of their homeland as the Spaniards had done during the Napoleonic invasion of 1808. He concluded that Mexico's military fiasco in 1847 could only be attributed to the fact that "there has not been, nor could there have been, a national spirit, for there is no nation."[11]

Unlike Otero, who wrote as the war neared its conclusion and looked back at Mexican society and its institutions, José Fernando Ramírez wrote as events transpired between December 1845 and September 1847, and in so doing authored what a twentieth-century author deemed the "best portrayal of Mexican domestic life" for that period.[12] A noted scholar who became involved in national affairs during the 1840s after holding various government posts in his home state of Durango during the preceding decade, Ramírez' collection of private memoranda and letters to Francisco Elorriaga, another

Nineteenth-century historian José Fernando Ramírez believed the moderado political faction hurt Mexico's chances of winning the war. Historians today have come to agree with his assessment of partisan problems. (From Vicente de Palacio ed., México a través de los siglos, México, 1884-1889, V. 1)

Durango politician, were posthumously published in 1905 by historian Genaro García as Mexico During the War with the United States. Ramírez' writings make clear that he regarded the turbulent factionalism that afflicted Mexican politics in the mid-nineteenth century as the main culprit for the debacle of 1847.[13]

While Ramírez' account criticizes politicians of all stripes, he first censured the *moderado* administration of Gen. José Joaquín de Herrera, characterizing it as "the symbol of ineptitude in politics."[14] That regime took power in December 1844 with the support of the diverse groups that made up the Mexican political spectrum at the time. All factions agreed that Gen. Antonio López de Santa Anna—who one year earlier had installed a personalistic dictatorship under the auspices of a constitution commonly known as the *Bases Orgánicas*—had to be removed from office. That backing had disappeared by mid-1845 largely as a result of Herrera's pacifist policies toward rebellious Texas, which allowed many to condemn his regime as "weak, vacillating, and cowardly."[15] In addition, Ramírez believed that the conduct of influential *moderado* statesman Manuel Gómez Pedraza had greatly contributed to the Herrera government's problems. He characterized Gómez Pedraza as nothing but "a mere child" when it came to "the most significant feature of politics: that of managing and knowing men," and blamed him for "having withdrawn [from public affairs] at the wrong time and in not knowing how to maintain the influence he once had."[16] The writings of the *moderado* mouthpiece *El Siglo XIX* also infuriated Ramírez. When its editors announced late in December 1845 that they planned to shut down the daily as Gen. Mariano Paredes y Arrillaga's effort to unseat Herrera grew more potent, Ramírez commented that *El Siglo XIX* had "done an immense amount of harm by confusing public opinion without furnishing adequate information and by encouraging anarchy."[17]

Ramírez subsequently continued to criticize the *moderados* for their personal selfishness rather than their incapacity once the radicals (or *puros*) took power early in August 1846. He lambasted the *moderado* attempt to block the installation of an advisory board created that month to foster political unity and counsel the government on the nation's problems. Key *moderado* statesmen who had pledged to serve the government went "back on their honorable commitments" and "hurriedly resigned" from the council. The first to do so was Gómez Pedraza, whose behavior angered Ramírez "not so much because it affects me personally, but because of the frightful future it prepares for us." He added that those "men did not think about that [i.e. the future]. Or perhaps they were incapable of foreseeing such a development." At the same time, however, Ramírez did not mince words about the goals and tactics employed by the *puros*. He chastised them for their intolerance, specifically their desire to enact "a clean sweep of state governments and assemblies to rid them" of opposing political factions. The enmity and jealousy that characterized relations between these two factions had, by early April 1847, caused Ramírez to lose faith in "the continuation of the representative system." It had fallen "into an abyss of infamy and lack of confidence" from which it was not likely to reemerge unscathed.[18]

Ramírez may have intended his comments to remain private, but Carlos María Bustamante had every intention of revealing his innermost thoughts in *El nuevo Bernal Díaz del Castillo, o sea, historia de la invasión de los Anglo-Americanos en México.* This acute observer of public life in early republican Mexico (the collection of his works covers 19,142 pages) authored his volume so "readers one hundred years from now could see what had transpired in Mexico" between 1845 and 1847.[19] A native of Oaxaca state who served as a deputy in seven different congresses between 1813 and 1837 as well as on the Supreme Conservative Power (a fourth branch of government under the 1836 centralist constitution), Bustamante's account directed its frustration at one man—General Santa Anna—and accused him of handing over the country to the U.S.

Bustamante's allegation rested on the conduct of U.S. commodore David E. Conner, who had failed to prevent Santa

Anna, who the Herrera administration had exiled to Cuba in May 1845, from evading the U.S. blockade of the Mexican Gulf coast and landing in Vera Cruz in August 1846. He also pointed to the fact that a U.S. commissioner then accompanied Santa Anna to his hacienda at El Encerro to draft a preliminary peace treaty.[20] Such connivance, in Bustamante's opinion, underscored many of Santa Anna's tactical and strategic military errors. He bitterly denounced Santa Anna and held him responsible for the Mexican army's "disorderly, precipitous, and disastrous retreat" following the Feb. 22-23, 1847, battle of Buena Vista. Not only did the withdrawal cost the nation a significant amount of men, money, and military equipment, but in addition Santa Anna had failed to obtain "any kind of advantage" from the encounter and had lied about the battle's results with consequent "discredit to his personal character and military honor."[21] Bustamante also harshly censured other battlefield choices made by Santa Anna. These included his failure to properly strengthen the Mexican defenses at the disastrous April 1847 battle of Cerro Gordo and his decision to order Gen. Anastasio Parrodi to abandon the eastern port of Tampico, destroy the forts that defended that plaza, and dump 670 muskets in the river despite the pleas of municipal leaders and the city's inhabitants not to do so.

Carlos María Bustamante believed General Santa Anna delivered Mexico to the United States, a pervasive view in Mexico today. Many modern historians, however, doubt this charge. (From Vicente de Palacio ed., México a través de los siglos, México, 1884-1889, V. 4)

In Bustamante's opinion, the only logical explanation for those occurrences was that the person who issued such orders was "a *traitor* in collusion with the enemy."[22]

Bustamante also found fault with Santa Anna's incessant political maneuvering. Given that public opinion remained suspicious about the Mexican general's political ambitions following his 1846 arrival in Vera Cruz, Santa Anna quickly moved to earn his countrymen's trust and to dispel all hints of complicity with the foreign foe. He issued a manifesto in mid-August which stated that he only wished to retake "the enviable title of soldier of the people" and "defend the republic's independence and liberty until his death." Santa Anna reiterated that sentiment just a few days prior to his triumphant re-entry into Mexico City on Sept. 14, 1846, when he stated that it would be "most degrading" to hold the presidency when duty called him to fight the enemies of the nation. He would thus immediately take charge of the army.[23] Bustamante considered such rhetoric nothing more than "an astute and political blow" that would allow Santa Anna to "dominate the people, subdue them to his will, and control them through the force of arms."[24] Santa Anna had to wait a few months, but by April 1847 he had fulfilled Bustamante's prophecy and managed to consolidate his grasp over Mexican politics.

The last of the four works under consideration, the collaborative production headed by Ramón Alcaraz entitled *Apuntes para la historia de la guerra entre México y los Estados Unidos* and first published in mid-August 1848,[25] nearly was lost to post-war censorship. Because many Mexicans still held Santa Anna at least partly responsible for the military defeat of 1847 and the ensuing loss of territory, during his last regime (1853-1855) Santa Anna tried to erase from public memory any events concerning the war with the U.S. For example, in mid-October 1853 his government characterized as "ridiculous" the drama *Los Yankees en el Valle de*

México (The Yankees in the Valley of Mexico) and banned theaters in Mexico City from staging the performance.[26] Santa Anna directed his ire toward Alcaraz and his fellow authors four months later. A mid-February 1854 directive dismissed them from any government posts they might hold, and also called for the removal of all issues of *Apuntes* from libraries, printing houses, and individual homes; all copies were then to be burnt in public. Some of Alcaraz' tomes, however, survived the onslaught, allowing scholars to examine a work that claimed to view the conflict with "impartiality."[27]

While *Apuntes* mainly focuses on military aspects of the struggle, early on its authors make a bold statement that remains illustrative of Mexican perspectives about the war; they indicted the U.S. as the aggressor and identified U.S. expansionism as a cause of the conflict. In their opinion, the "true origin of the war" lay in the U.S.' "insatiable ambition" and in its desire "to extend their dominion in such a manner as to become the absolute owners of almost all this continent."[28] The Alcaraz volume is also noteworthy because it is the only one of the four under review that evaluates—although briefly—the Treaty of Guadalupe Hidalgo, the 1848 accord that ended the war. Alcaraz and his co-authors synthesized the pro-peace and pro-war arguments "advanced by [Manuel de la] Peña y Peña and [Manuel Crescencio] Rejón respectively, but they refrained both from commenting on the treaty itself and from revealing their own position on the debate."[29] The authors claimed that three reasons guided their decision: the desire not to substitute criticisms for narrative, an inability to be impartial due to sadness over the war's outcome, and the diversity of opinions among them on the question of war and peace.[30] The enormous dissatisfaction that the treaty had generated by mid-1848 most likely also influenced their silence, for to express any kind of opinion on the subject would have heightened political tensions even further. The terms of the accord had already provided an opportunistic regular army officer, the aforementioned General Paredes, with a pretext to lead a short-lived uprising against the Herrera regime shortly after it returned to power in early June 1848,[31] while a number of journalists blamed the *moderado* administrations that had engaged in peace negotiations with the U.S. for generating the social ills that beleaguered Mexico City and the country at large.[32]

★★★

Latter-day historians who have analyzed the U.S.-Mexican War have found the assessments of Otero, Ramírez, Bustamante, and Alcaraz both convincing and well founded. Otero's notions concerning the absence of a sense of nationhood seem largely accurate. His opinion of the Mexican military has been corroborated by William A. DePalo Jr.'s recent monograph on the development of the Mexican army in the three decades that followed independence. DePalo's work explains how Mexico's political struggles, chronic indebtedness, Indian raids, rivalries between generals, and a popular disdain for military service obstructed the efforts of Mexican statesmen and military reformers to professionalize the army and bring it under civilian control. These conditions, according to DePalo, led to the emergence of an ill-trained and badly provisioned conscript army that could not repel various foreign threats to the nation's sovereignty, particularly that from the U.S.[33]

Michael P. Costeloe has also confirmed Otero's assertions concerning the Catholic Church's determination to protect its own interests rather than Mexico's during the 1846-1848 conflict. Upset that in mid-January 1847 Valentín Gómez Farías, the acting *puro* chief executive, had issued a decree authorizing the government to raise 15 million pesos for the war effort by mortgaging or selling Church property, clerical leaders reacted by financing the so-called "rebellion of the *polkos*" against the regime. The uprising, which erupted in Mexico City late that February and continued for nearly a month, coincided with the landing of Gen. Winfield Scott's expeditionary army in Vera Cruz, and prevented the government, which had to confront the *polko* rebels, from coming to the defense of the port city. Barbara Tenembaum has echoed this assessment of the Church's self-centered stance, suggesting that as negotiators hammered out the 1848 peace settlement members of the upper clergy sought peace and advocated that the U.S. absorb Mexico so the Church could keep its property. Historians, nonetheless, should further probe Tenembaum's allegation given the meager evidence—one letter written by Nicholas P. Trist, the chief U.S. architect of the 1848 peace agreement—that supports it.[34]

Otero's assessment of the factors that profoundly impacted Mexico's ability to meet the foreign threat did not consider regionalism, one of the most forceful phenomena in nineteenth-century Mexican history. The process whereby colonial New Spain disintegrated into the constituent regions that comprised the Mexican republic commenced in earnest during the final decades of the eighteenth century with the establishment of the intendancy system by the Bourbon monarchs. It continued into the early 1800s with the creation of provincial deputations and the deterioration of Mexico's war of independence into a series of local insurgencies. Regionalism strengthened the leaders of many peripheral areas who then obstructed the efforts of the Mexico City-based political elite to rule the new republic. In doing so they turned provincialism into "the foremost driving force of the early period following independence."[35]

The pervasiveness of regionalism in early republican Mexico all but ensured that in the mid-1840s many states and other local entities would focus on "their immediate problems, [and] relegate the problem of the war [with the U.S.] to a secondary level."[36] For example, in the fall of 1846 state authorities frustrated the central government's efforts to deploy national guard units in the struggle against the U.S. Several governors, anxious to preserve local leadership and provincial autonomy, publicly protested when the federal government tried to take command of those forces.[37] Not even the advance of U.S. troops into Mexico's heartland the following summer prompted state authorities like Guanajuato chief executive Lorenzo Arellano to provide military assistance to the central government. He argued that according to the 1824 federal constitution (which had been re-enacted in mid-September 1846) "the president of the Republic cannot dispose of the states' local militia without the consent of Congress, nor can Congress give it unless it specifically states the number of men; but never in a vague and undetermined manner." Arellano added that without the support of the national guard Guanajuato's government would be unable to resist the "despotic power" of those individuals who threatened federalism as well the bandits and thieves who marauded on the roads, stole cattle, and pillaged villages. He concluded that Guanajuato's economy would be devastated if the national guard left the state because most guardsmen were married, had a family, and had established themselves in agriculture, commerce, or mining.[38] Such constitutional, political, and economic arguments were only a facade; as José Fernando Ramírez noted, "even a fifteen year old girl is not as precise in matters of honor as these states are in respect to their inflated sovereignty."[39]

Other reasons beyond regionalism also contributed to Mexico's military fiasco. Timothy D. Johnson's recent biography of Gen. Winfield Scott showcases Scott's brilliance as a field commander and tactician, attributes that became particularly evident during the 1847 Mexico City campaign, an undertaking that military authorities like the Duke of Wellington considered impossible. The man who defeated Napoleon Bonaparte at the 1815 Battle of Waterloo assessed Scott's situation early in the summer of 1847 and remarked: "Scott is lost ... He can't take the city [Mexico], and he can't fall back upon his base [Vera Cruz]."[40] According to Johnson, Scott triumphed in Mexico because he relied on flanking movements to avoid bloody engagements and minimize casualties, and also since he drew upon his past military experiences and the lessons of history. His inability to wage an effective guerrilla war against the Seminole Indians in the 1830s, as well as the irregular partisan warfare and political disorder that doomed Napoleon's efforts to control Spain during the Peninsular War (1808-1814), influenced his decision to impose martial law in Mexico in the spring of 1847 to avoid a protracted insurgency. The success of Scott's pacification plan should encourage historians to challenge the axiom that Mexicans did not rise up in defense of their homeland simply because of a lack of national spirit.[41]

Just like Ramírez avowed nearly one hundred and sixty years ago, recent research has demonstrated that Mexican statesmen failed to put aside partisan interests in the face of a foreign invasion. According to Timothy Anna, by the mid-1800s Mexican political elites had embarked upon a course of self-destruction reminiscent of actions attributed to Roman emperor Nero. As he put it, "not only did they [the politicians] fiddle while Rome [Mexico City] burned, but the more it burned the faster they fiddled."[42] Both Miguel Soto and Jaime Delgado have emphasized a vital component of this destructive process, the Spanish intrigue to restore monarchy to Mexico during the mid-1840s. Headed by the Spanish minister in Mexico, Salvador Bermúdez de Castro, and aided by the country's pre-eminent conservative thinker and politician, Lucas Alamán, the conspirators convinced General Paredes to take supreme power, convene a congress in which Mexico's most conservative thinkers would prevail, and invite Spain to provide a monarch. Stationed in San Luis Potosí in mid-December 1845 with an army several thousand strong poised to advance north to Texas, Paredes instead marched south to Mexico City, deposed Herrera, and installed himself as chief executive.[43] Other scholars have illustrated additional reasons that contributed to instability that prevailed in Mexico at the time. In both the capital and in many states members of the four major factions that had struggled for political supremacy since the early nineteenth-century—radicals (or *puros*), moderates (or *moderados*), conservatives, and *santanistas*—could not put aside partisan interests, and continued to clash over issues such as the role of the Catholic Church and the regular army, along with the participation of the lower classes in public affairs.[44]

Bustamante's negative appraisal of General Santa Anna's role in the U.S.-Mexican War is one of the most lasting legacies left by post-war Mexican authors. Although Ramírez, historian José María Roa Bárcena, and the noted essayist Guillermo Prieto—to name but three prominent nineteenth-century authors—have rejected Bustamante's characterization of Santa Anna as a traitor,[45] to this day official Mexican history demonizes Santa Anna and holds him responsible for many of the troubles that befell the country in the three decades that followed independence, including the calamitous war with the U.S. In 1996 I participated in a roundtable in Mexico City's *Museo Nacional de las Intervenciones* to commemorate the sesquicentennial of the commencement of hostilities. During the question-and-answer period, a member of the audience seriously asked the following question: "Who is the greater traitor—Santa Anna or Carlos Salinas de Gortari [president of Mexico, 1988-1994]?" In addition, the titles of two recent biographies emphasize that some modern-day historians remain convinced that Santa Anna was either a traitor or the individual to be blamed for Mexico's misfortunes: Héctor Díaz Zermeño's *La culminación de las traiciones de Santa Anna* and Robert Scheina's *Santa Anna: A Curse Upon Mexico.*[46]

A number of historians, however, have insisted that Santa Anna was neither as disloyal nor incompetent as Bustamante and others have claimed. Enrique Krause, one of Mexico's leading popular non-fiction authors, argues in a mammoth volume that traces Mexico's history through the lives of its leaders that Santa Anna would "have been granted a place in Mexican history as a hero or perhaps as a martyr" had he died after his 1829 victory over the Spanish at Tampico, or after repulsing the French in Vera Cruz in 1838, or even after the 1836 debacle at San Jacinto and the setbacks during the war with the U.S. As Krause notes, "up until 1847 everybody thought of him [Santa Anna] as the savior of the nation. The vices and virtues that so marked him were not his alone but those of the Mexican people who incessantly sought him out and welcomed him, cheered and cursed him. Every Mexican, on more than one occasion, had been a follower of Santa Anna."[47]

Other scholars have rejected traditional categorizations of early nineteenth-century Mexican politics that ascribe to the Santa Anna an indispensable role in such affairs; Enrique González Pedrero's *País de un solo hombre: El México de Santa Anna*, published in 1993 by the prominent Mexico City publisher Fondo de Cultura Económica, is a recent example of this trend. In *Mexico in the Age of Proposals (1821-1853)*, Will Fowler argues that the era can be more accurately assessed if dissected into several stages: hope (1821-1828), disenchantment (1828-1835), profound disillusion (1836-1847), and despair (1847-1855).[48] In addition, Fowler's biographical study of Gen. José María Tornel y Mendívil, the *santanistas'* (as Santa Anna's adherents were known) main adviser and public spokesman, helps explain how and why Santa Anna took power time and again. A prolific and well-regarded author, Tornel's speeches and writings repeatedly rehabilitated Santa Anna's public image because they portrayed him as a true patriot who only intervened in politics for the good of the country. As a result, Santa

Anna was able to secure the army's favor and salvage his reputation as a leading general following military disasters like the Texas campaign of 1836 and the U.S.-Mexican War of 1846-1848.[49]

Scholars have also reappraised Santa Anna's military skills. As one writer pointed out, DePalo's study of the Mexican army made it possible "for the first time … to assess whether Santa Anna … was a good general or not."[50] The book offers an earnest analysis of the battles of Buena Vista and Cerro Gordo that discounts treason as the explanation for the outcome of the two encounters. In DePalo's opinion, Santa Anna "acquitted himself reasonably well" at Buena Vista, but the battle turned into a "succession of small-unit actions in which individual initiative and the tactical and technical acumen of leaders acting on their own volition were keys to success." These circumstances put Santa Anna and the Mexican army at a disadvantage because "American junior officers were infinitely better prepared than their Mexican counterparts." Likewise, DePalo writes off treason as the reason for the U.S. rout of the Mexican army at Cerro Gordo. In this case, he argues, Santa Anna's poor generalship greatly contributed to the debacle. Not only did Santa Anna choose "piecemeal, non-mutually supporting defensive positions against the advice of his chief engineer officer," but he also failed to account for the effects of the region's hot climate, which subjected Mexican troops to "insect infestation, water shortages, and inadequate provisions" that "exacerbated morale problems" among them.[51]

Bustamante's memoir did not cover the Mexico City campaign, but doubtlessly he would have found ample fault with Santa Anna's maneuvers to further advance the charge of treason. Scheina's assessment of the battles for the Mexican capital, however, precludes such a judgment. He not only praised Santa Anna for his "tireless energy" in recruiting soldiers, but also complimented him for the soundness of the defensive scheme he devised late in the summer of 1847 to protect the city. According to Scheina, Santa Anna supplemented the natural defenses that geography had bestowed on the capital with a number of man-made fortifications. He also noted that because the army raised by Santa Anna was "so ill prepared that it could not execute offensive maneuvers," the Mexican general "wisely ... chose a defensive strategy whereby he would man the strong-points with the inexperienced national guard units and employ his regulars as a mobile reserve." Scheina then reviewed the encounters between the opposing armies in and around the capital, and concluded that Santa Anna was "not entirely to blame for Mexico's catastrophe."[52]

What to make of Alcaraz' charges concerning the origins of the war? A number of historians have characterized the concept of Manifest Destiny, as New York journalist John L. O'Sullivan labeled in mid-1845 the U.S. desire to expand across the North American continent, as merely an elaborate rationale for aggressive land acquisition. Such assessments, however, have failed to consider the setting in which it developed. According to Richard Bruce Winders, Manifest Destiny corresponded with the ideological and intellectual trends of the late eighteenth century, and was "very real to post-Revolutionary War citizens of the new republic called the United States of America."[53] Indeed, as Randy Roberts and James S. Olson have noted, in the mid-1830s the Texas rebels constantly made reference to the vocabulary of the American Revolution to rationalize the uprising against Mexican rule. These men, "like the Americans of the Revolutionary era, who claimed that George III and Parliament had violated their God-given rights as English subjects, ... felt that General Santa Anna had done the same."[54] And as James E. Crisp has shown, the fighting in Texas began not over "culturally sensitive questions of language, religion, race, or slavery, but rather over issues that divided so many other frontier areas of Mexico from the central government:

91

disagreement over states' rights and local autonomy; exorbitant tariffs and the haphazard suppression of smuggling; inefficient and arbitrary administration of the laws; and the weakness and corruption of the army."[55] The opinions of Winders, Roberts and Olson, and Crisp suggest, therefore, that Alcaraz' estimation of the U.S.' "spirit of aggrandizement" as the "real and effective cause" of the conflict ought to be tempered.[56]

On the other hand, the preeminent diplomatic historian Piero Gleijeses recently shed new light on Alcaraz' assertion that the U.S. deliberately provoked war with Mexico. Gleijeses notes that scholars have focused on John Slidell's 1845-1846 diplomatic mission to Mexico to settle damage claims as well as to possibly purchase California and New Mexico as the litmus test for whether or not U.S. President James K. Polk purposely sought to goad Mexico into war.[57] The attention that historians have given to this question (which Gleijeses asserts cannot be answered conclusively) has led them to neglect another theme that takes on the matter of U.S. responsibility for the conflict—the silence that preceded Polk's May 11, 1846, war message to Congress. Was the president's belligerent policy prior to the outbreak of hostilities "so stealthy that no one could see the drift to war?" To answer this query Gleijeses measured U.S. public opinion through an examination of twelve U.S. dailies from mid-1845 to mid-1846 that represented a variety of political and geographic perspectives, and concluded that these newspapers "paid very little attention to Mexico ... [which] was a sideshow [to the Oregon dispute]." Consequently, the U.S. media never adequately explained why two Mexican governments failed to receive Slidell, and they practically ignored Gen. Zachary Taylor's advance to the Rio Grande, a move that made war all but inevitable. Likewise, Gleijeses notes that Congress remained silent about Polk's policies before war broke out because its members "paid even less attention to Mexico than did the press." These findings led Gleijeses to conclude that the stillness with which the U.S. greeted Polk as he marched to war was not because the country "thought it was moral, but because it thought it would be easy."[58]

★★★

While scholars have analyzed the perspectives put forth by Otero, Ramírez, Bustamante, and Alcaraz more than one hundred fifty years ago, since 1996 academics have begun to explore several heretofore-neglected aspects of the war with emphasis on Mexican domestic matters. One area concerns Mexican guerrilla operations. Alcaraz, Ramírez, and Bustamante each discussed the prospects of Mexico undertaking a guerrilla war against the U.S., but they did not present a systematic analysis of this possibility. Alcaraz briefly described the most notable achievements of guerrilla operations, Bustamante expressed faith in the guerrillas' potential to disrupt U.S. forces, and Ramírez lacked confidence in the long-range potential for success of guerrilla warfare.[59] Likewise, a 1969 monograph by Günter Kahle failed to offer any critical insights about the topic. Chapter III of his work focused on guerrilla warfare in nineteenth-century Mexico, but only four of its 34 pages covered the war with the U.S., and they merely described the most important of the twenty-seven articles of an April 1847 decree issued by the regime of Gen. Pedro María Anaya that tried to standardize guerrilla operations.[60]

Thanks to Irving W. Levinson, however, this significant aspect of the war has found a historian to reveal its intricacies. Levinson's recent *Wars within War: Mexican Guerrillas, Domestic Elites, and the United States of America, 1846-1848* characterizes the war between Mexico and the U.S. not only as a conflict between two sovereign nations, but also as a struggle between white and indigenous Mexicans, between the U.S. army and Mexican guerrillas, and between those Americans opposed to the war and President Polk. One of Levinson's key points is that the Mexican guerrillas that emerged during the war forced the Mexican state to abandon any hopes for a protracted struggle against the U.S. army, as government officials instead chose to "refocus military efforts upon restoring their own hegemony." Levinson further notes that guerrilla warfare convinced the U.S. to abandon its quest for territory in northern Mexico. Before the conflict U.S. statesmen like Secretary of State James Buchanan had "considered the twenty-sixth parallel to be the appropriate post-war boundary." Such a border would have included the present-day Mexican states of Chihuahua and Sonora, as well as large parts of Baja California, Coahuila, Tamaulipas, and Nuevo León. Partisan resistance in Mexico, however, forced the U.S. government to abandon its quest to possess these lands.[61]

If Levinson's book illuminates the activities of many of the nameless guerrillas who roamed the countryside and resisted foreign interlopers, the work of Luis Fernando Granados performs a similar function for Mexico City's urban poor. Building on recent scholarship that has stressed the role of the urban popular classes as key historical actors during the turbulent post-independence era, in *Sueñan las piedras: Alzamiento ocurrido en la ciudad de México, 14, 15, y 16 de septiembre de 1847* Granados examines the three-day mid-September 1847 riot by Mexico City's so-called "masses" against General Scott and the U.S. expeditionary army and rejects the conventional notion that anti-U.S. feelings prompted the confrontation. Instead, Granados portrays the rebellion as a massive and spontaneous social movement, largely driven by the growing involvement of the poor in public affairs and by governmental policies that worsened their living conditions as war approached the capital. Their plight ruptured the loyalty of the poor to Mexican authorities and led them to resist Scott's forces.

After an introductory chapter that places the work within the historiography of the U.S.-Mexican War, Granados explains how the defeats suffered by Mexican troops in the battles and skirmishes of Sept. 13 fostered a sense of uneasiness among city residents that set the stage for the riot. By midnight not only had the Mexican army withdrawn from the capital and the town council (*ayuntamiento*) disbanded the national guard, leaving the city defenseless, but bandits had also begun to loot the National Palace. Then, the indifference with which the multitude of poor Mexicans who gathered in the central plaza (*Zócalo*) as dawn broke on the 14th to observe U.S. forces hoist the Stars and Stripes added to the situation's volatility. The assembled crowd only saw bedraggled soldiers, not the invincible men described by several Mexican observers as U.S. troops had made their way inland.

These realities drove the urban poor to attack, within a few hours, the occupying U.S. soldiers with stones, bottles, and other loose objects. Although Granados cannot ascertain the insurrection's starting point or the specific incident that triggered it, he explains that the riot was centered in lower-class neighborhoods such as Santa Catarina and Santa Ana. Residents of wealthy districts, like those who lived on Plateros Street, abstained from fighting and hung flags from foreign nations from their homes' balconies in an attempt to avoid the commotion. Granados also finds most of the rebellion's leaders to have been mid-level political activists like Francisco Próspero Pérez, a radical (*puro*) militant, or individuals with much popular appeal such as Celedonio Jarauta, a Spanish priest who had arrived in Mexico in 1844 and emerged as a proficient guerrilla fighter in the state of Vera Cruz during the spring of 1847. Surviving accounts do not even suggest that any member of Mexico's upper and middle-class spearheaded an effort to drive out U.S. troops.[62]

Cultural historians of Latin America have recently turned much attention on the creation of national identity and ways in which the region's regimes have put national values on view.[63] In the case of Mexico, scholars have explored how that country's early nineteenth-century governments moved in cultural ways to legitimize the government and turn the former Spanish colonists into citizens of the new nation. Among other things, the regimes instituted holidays and celebrations honoring their independence heroes, Father Miguel Hidalgo y Costilla and Gen. Agustín de Iturbide among others.[64] General Santa Anna also made use of public ceremonies while in power to foster the general public's loyalty to the state as well as to remind people of his own importance to the country. He added the anniversary of his Sept. 11, 1829, victory over Spanish troops at Tampico to the calendar of festivities, and in 1842 staged a funeral for the leg lost four years earlier during the so-called Pastry War versus France.[65]

Likewise, historians have studied the civic rituals used by public-spirited Mexicans in the aftermath of the U.S.-Mexican War to consolidate the authority of the state and build a sense of nationhood. Enrique Plascencia de la Parra analyzed one of Mexico's most cherished myths and best-known symbols of national solidarity, that of the so-called *Niños Héroes*. According to legend, six cadets from the national military academy (*Colegio Militar*) who in September 1847 helped to defend Chapultepec Castle against U.S. forces chose to die rather than surrender to their adversaries. One of the cadets, Juan Escutia, reputedly wrapped the Mexican flag around his body and jumped over the battlements to his death. De la Parra shows that the heroic young boys lapsed from the national historical memory for approximately twenty-five years, but that the patriotic euphoria that accompanied Mexico's victory over the French invaders in 1867 set the groundwork for the cadets' subsequent commemoration as national heroes. Beginning in 1871 and continuing throughout the twentieth century, a host of Mexican military organizations and government officials reworked the legend to fulfill their own particular agendas.

For decades, the story of Juan Escutia wrapping himself in a Mexican flag and jumping to his death from the walls of Chapultepec Castle rather than surrendering to Americans was a symbol of Mexican solidarity. (Pastel by Charles Colley courtesy of the University of Texas at Arlington Library Special Collections)

Especially significant in this regard were the efforts of the Porfirio Díaz regime (1876-1911), which within ten years of assuming power promoted the cult of the *Niños Héroes* as the epitome of loyalty, honor, and patriotic duty.[66]

In exalting the *Niños Héroes*, however, Mexican official rhetoric and ritual all but forgot the heroism of a number of real flesh-and-blood heroes who sacrificed their lives in the war with the U.S. Many of these individuals belonged to the *polko* national guard battalions that helped defend Mexico City in the summer of 1847, and recent research has demonstrated how in the aftermath of war

General Herrera and his *moderado* cohorts heralded and utilized their bravery in an effort to construct a useful past from the memories of the debacle. Between 1848 and 1850 Herrera's administration staged public ceremonies in their honor to alleviate the pain of defeat, bring together a divided nation, and reorganize the national guard into a military force manned by the well-to-do that would help preserve political stability and social harmony. For this purpose they chose a number of valiant national guardsmen, of whom Lucas Balderas today holds the most prominent place in the Mexican collective memory.[67]

A well-known tailor and important popular politician in the early republic, Balderas served as colonel of the *"Mina"* national guard battalion that helped defend the Molino del Rey, a building complex located some two miles southwest of the capital and one thousand yards west of Chapultepec Castle where General Scott thought that Santa Anna was collecting church bells and having them cast into cannon. Believing he needed to take the compound to capture Mexico City, Scott launched an attack during the early morning of Sept. 8.

Col. Lucas Balderas, a national guardsman who died fighting valiantly at Molino del Rey, holds the most prominent place today among heroes in the Mexican collective memory. (From Vicente de Palacio ed., México a través de los siglos, México, 1884-1889, V. 4)

Balderas demonstrated exemplary military audacity, selflessness, and patriotism during the course of the battle. Shortly after hostilities commenced, Balderas, mounted on a steed, suffered a leg wound that bled profusely. Nonetheless, he remained on his horse and led a charge to retake artillery pieces captured by U.S. forces. A cannon ball struck Balderas as he advanced, but his combativeness did not desert him. Brandishing his sword, Balderas continued to fight on one knee until four of his men carried him from the battlefield to a nearby hut. There, as he expired in the arms of his son, Balderas inquired about the status of the battle. His poignant last words were said to have been: "My poor country!"[68]

Given Balderas' heroics, as well as the fact that many of his contemporaries believed he possessed the most pure public spirit, government officials and public-spirited citizens conferred upon him a prominent place in the pantheon of Mexican heroes and memorialized him in various ways from the time of first anniversary of the battle of Molino del Rey through the late 1860s. These honors included solemn memorial services, a posthumous promotion to artillery colonel in the regular army, naming a Mexico City-based national guard regiment after him, the internment of his ashes in a monument that commemorated the combatants of Molino del Rey, and naming one the capital's most important streets in his honor. To this day Balderas remains a constant presence in the Mexican collective memory. One of the stops of Line 3 of Mexico City's subway system, which traverses the capital from the National University (UNAM) in the south to Indios Verdes in the north, is named in his honor; an artillery cannon pictorially represents the station. In addition, public officials in Balderas' hometown of San Miguel de Allende continue to remember their native son. Every Sept. 8 local political and cultural leaders sponsor a commemorative service at the city's main plaza that pays homage to this heroic Mexican.[69]

★★★

The continued resonance of the memory of the U.S.-Mexican War in contemporary Mexico is perhaps best illustrated by the fact that a number of associations and individuals who have tried to challenge the status quo have relied on the symbols that emerged from the conflict to press their views. In 1997, a deputy for the left-wing *Partido de la Revolución Democrática* (PRD), Gilberto López Rivas, criticized the *Partido Revolucionario Institucional* (PRI), which in its various incarnations held power in Mexico between 1929 and 2000, for the way it had commemorated the hundred and fiftieth anniversary of the Sept. 13, 1847, battle of Chapultepec. According to López Rivas, the president's envoy did not speak about the war but rather used the opportunity to promote the neoliberal project favored by the Ernesto Zedillo administration. The Mexican legislator found it "unacceptable to pay homage to the *Niños Héroes* of Chapultepec by offering to perpetuate an economic policy that had increased the number of hungry and persecuted street children as well as the number of indigenous children who remain marginalized from progress."[70]

Recent developments, however, suggest that legends such as the *Niños Héroes* will no longer form part of the nation's official historic discourse. In the summer of 2005 Mexico's National History Museum, which is located in Chapultepec Castle and welcomes an average of ten thousand visitors a day (and even more on Sundays, when entrance is free), finished a thorough reorganization of its permanent exhibits. The displays no longer showcase the country's most relevant historical events in chronological or sequential fashion, but rather in a thematic and conceptual manner. In keeping with the modification, museum officials removed from the main passageway those objects and ideas that did not conform to the new vision, including everything that referred to the *Niños Héroes* (such paraphernalia is now found in a small and rather unpretentious room).[71] To further underscore the fresh outlook, one of the museum's curators, Víctor Manuel Ruíz, informed journalists that no young cadet leaped to his death with the Mexican flag wrapped around him.[72]

Members of Mexico's intellectual elite may be devoting much time and effort to rendering a more accurate (as they see it) and nuanced portrayal of their country's history. This does not mean, however, that the public will forget the *Niños Héroes* or debunk the myth, nor does it imply that the resentments that emerged and crystallized as a result of the war with the U.S. will vanish. Mexico's National History Museum continues to exhibit the regimental flag of the New Orleans Grays, which Mexican forces captured during the 1836 siege of the Alamo. Years ago, when current U.S. President George W. Bush ran for governor of Texas, he made recovery of that flag one of his campaign promises; officials in his administration have continued such efforts, even offering to trade Santa Anna's wooden leg (which U.S. forces captured as the Mexican general fled the Cerro Gordo battlefield and now forms part of the collection of the Illinois National Guard and Militia Historical Society) in its stead.[73] Curator Ruíz replied that Mexicans had no interest in any such exchange. He said that Mexico already had Santa Anna's other leg, and added—with a touch of national pride likely intended to badger U.S. sensibilities—that flags cannot be returned because they are considered war trophies.[74] Ruíz' remarks, while representative of one man's opinion, strongly suggest that the aftershocks of the 1846-1848 conflict will continue to resonate for the foreseeable future.

The *Other* War
That Remade America

By Elliott West

The Mexican War has my vote as our most nearly forgotten conflict. The Spanish-American War and the War of 1812 are contenders, but the first at least left us with "Remember the Maine!" and the Rough Riders on San Juan (actually Kettle) Hill, while the other gave us the national anthem. But the Mexican War? There's the opening line of the "Marine Hymn" ("From the halls of Montezuma ...."), but even many who know it are unlikely to identify it with Gen. Winfield Scott's men storming Mexico City. The whole business is pretty much a blank spot in American memory. Stop ten people on the street and I will bet that one at most will remember the Mexican War at all, and that person probably will be pretty fuzzy on when and why it happened and what it has meant to us.

That's too bad, for two reasons. First, Mexico, our neighbor and essential partner in hemispheric relations, has not forgotten. Some in that country consider the Mexican War the greatest calamity in their history. In the Treaty of Guadalupe Hidalgo (1848), Mexico lost roughly half its territory. Ask yourself: How would Americans feel if Britain or France had whipped us a century and a half ago and had taken everything east of a line from Lincoln, Nebraska, Tulsa, Oklahoma and Dallas, Texas, plus much of Alaska's fisheries and oil reserves? More generally the war produced a souring of relations to the south of us. Before the 1830s Latin American nations had revered the United States as the first colony to break free of its Old World master. After 1848 we were the great bully of the north.

102

With the Treaty of Guadalupe Hidalgo in 1848, the United States annexed about half of Mexico. Combined with the acquisition of Oregon as the war began, the land mass acquired was almost half again as big as the Louisiana Purchase. (Courtesy of the Arkansas History Commission)

The Mexican War, besides, was hugely important in our own history. That becomes especially clear when we consider the war's impact in its broadest context, the full implications for United States and North American history during the several generations that followed. In fact, I'll go further. If we consider the war part of a single larger episode, the acquisition of territory between 1845 and 1848, including the annexation of Texas and the acquisition of the Pacific Northwest, that great gulping of land rivaled in importance that *other* event of the mid-nineteenth century, the least-forgotten episode in American history, the Civil War.

The United States entered the twentieth century as essentially a new nation. It had emerged out of fundamental changes set loose in the middle years of the nineteenth century. When someone speaks of the transforming events of those years, we assume he is talking about the Civil War and the episodes around it. Obviously that war was enormously important for reasons starting with its volume of bloodshed and its freeing of four million slaves. But when we keep the larger picture in view, and when we keep in mind the course of our history in the twentieth century, the acquisition of the far West, with the Mexican War as its key event, should stand beside the Civil War in explaining what has happened. Saying it this way implies a competition between the two, a contest for a national championship belt for historical significance, heavyweight division. The point, rather, is that the Mexican and Civil Wars were partners in a national transformation. Far western expansion and the conflict of North and South resonated with one another. Together they produced the new American state.

Begin with land. The Mexican War, plus Texas and the country acquired from Great Britain in the Oregon Treaty (Oregon, Washington, Idaho and part of Montana), added up to nearly 1.2 million square miles, or more than 763 million acres. If these additions are considered interrelated parts of a single episode, this was far and away the greatest acquisition of territory in American history. It was nearly half again (144 percent) larger than the Louisiana Purchase. With the Gadsden Purchase of 1854, an after dinner mint following the great gorging of 1845-48, the "lower forty-eight" was complete. Such a development insists we ask some basic questions. What did adding that much land, specifically adding *that* land, mean to the course of American history? What were some of the consequences, in the short and the long run, for good and for ill? And how did those consequences help transform an earlier American republic into something fundamentally new?

104

One obvious answer concerns resources, and any discussion of that should open with the greatest coincidence in American history. On Jan. 24, 1848, gold was discovered along the American River in northern California. That famous find came just *nine days*, a bit more than two hundred hours, before the signing of the Treaty of Guadalupe Hidalgo in a suburb of Mexico City. At virtually the same moment that the United States acquired California, California began to be revealed as

The discovery of gold in California, just nine days before the treaty with Mexico, created towns like Sutter's Creek almost overnight. Gold was just one of the West's resources that fueled U.S. growth for decades. (Courtesy of the Library of Congress Prints and Photographs Division)

the richest real estate on Planet Earth. The amount of gold mined across the world between 1848 and 1858 surpassed the amount taken out from 1492 until 1848. Some of that gold came from elsewhere—there were strikes in Australia, for instance—but most by far came out of the hills we took from Mexico just as they began hemorrhaging money. Eventually California produced an estimated billion dollars (nineteenth-century dollars, remember) in gold. There followed a series of other gold and silver strikes, most of them in territory acquired between 1845 and 1848, including that of Nevada's Comstock Lode that comprised at that time the richest silver mines in history. Until ten years before the first strike there, the Comstock also was part of Mexico.

A fundamental step in making the new American state was its transition to an industrial economy. To call building that new economy "capital intensive" is masterly understatement. It was the most expensive undertaking in America history prior to World War

II, and just as the voracious need of capital for factories and cities was really being felt, the nation discovered that, with far westward expansion, it was literally sitting on a gold mine. Gold and silver were the most dazzling of our new resources, but there were many more. The most valuable non-precious metal for industrialization was copper used in making new machinery and in electrification. What for decades were the richest deposits in the world were at Butte in the Montana mountains and in Arizona. Industrialization and the explosive growth of cities relied on an expanding market agriculture to feed those leaving the American countryside. Farmlands acquired in the 1840s proved to be some of the richest anywhere, and quite early they also began to bring money into the nation by selling their produce to other nations. As early as the 1870s England's leading source of wheat was, amazingly, California, the state that today is the nation's agricultural powerhouse. In 1880 that state's wheat production was more than that of Kansas and Nebraska combined.[1]

Then there were the rangelands to raise cattle for increasingly beef-crazy urban markets and the sheep that gave their wool to textile mills. Constructing the physical plant for the new American state required almost unimaginable amounts of wood. Much came from other parts of the nation, the forests of Wisconsin for instance, but much, especially for reconstructing the far West, came from the timberlands of the Pacific Northwest and from forested regions of California and the Southwest. Harvesting western trees meshed with the new economy in ways that don't quickly come to mind. The Comstock mines, for example, were the deepest in the world. Shoring them up required eight hundred million board feet of lumber, enough to build fifty thousand modern ranch style houses, each with two baths and a two-car garage.[2] During the twentieth century other essential resources, such as uranium, would be found in the treasure house that had been northern Mexico.

An aphorism holds that God looks after dogs, drunks, and the United States of America. Considering what this nation has found in the lands acquired in the 1840s, and considering how much of that benefit was unpredicted, starting with the massive unbidden jolt of the most desired substance in history, that bit of folk wisdom carries a lot of weight. Without those resources there was simply no way the nation we know today could have emerged as it did and as rapidly as it did.

The war brought another addition, less obviously consequential than gold mines but hugely important—Pacific ports. Unlike gold, we knew what we were getting. The desire for ports had been a prime reason the United States had pushed Mexico into the conflict—and make no mistake: we were the aggressor. Our special need for Mexican ports had partly to do with differences between Pacific and Atlantic geographies. The Atlantic coast has been shaped largely by the pressing weight of ancient glaciers and the rising seawater after the end of the last ice age. As a result rivers flow into the Atlantic through country that is relatively low and flat, and their lower courses are flooded by the ocean well upriver—the famous tidewater region. For European colonizers that was happy news. It meant an abundance of ports and easy access to most of the coast. The great shaping force of the Pacific coast has been the grinding collision of tectonic plates. That has lifted the shoreline up. Today that makes for the spectacular scenery of places like Big Sur and breathtaking drives along California's famed U.S. Highway One, but earlier ships might sail for weeks along the Pacific coast without finding a place to land. Only two major rivers empty into the Pacific, and the mouth of one, the Columbia, was blocked by a series of shifting sandbars and tossed by frequent storms. Far from a welcoming harbor, it was an infamous graveyard for ships. That left basically four usable

*The valuable port of San Francisco was alluring to expansionist Americans with an eye
on trade in the Pacific well before the war. It became even more valuable with the gold
rush. (Courtesy of the Library of Congress Prints and Photographs Division)*

Pacific ports—at Puget Sound, San Diego, Monterey, and the
incomparable San Francisco Bay, the outlet of the Sacramento
River, the other major stream besides the Columbia.

Strategically and economically, then, each individual port took
on an extremely high value. And diplomatically, that left the
United States with a big problem: of the four ports listed above, all
but the first were in Mexico.[3]

American desire for Pacific ports tells us that even in the 1840s
some eastern interests were looking toward the far side of the
continent. Descriptions of California's interior valleys already
conjured up images of an agrarian mother lode. Those accounts
jibed with others from the Oregon country, especially the lands
south of the Columbia River, soil reportedly so fertile that, in an
overlander's phrase, you "can plant a nail and it'll come up a
spike." Should the republic's farmers leap to the Pacific, the most

practical connections back to their mother culture would be by sea, which made ports the connecting points between two widely separated centers of population.

More telling for the future, business interests in the Northeast were already calculating what they could do with trade connections to various points around the Pacific—to China, Japan, Australia and elsewhere. Such arrangements would require a fleet of merchant ships based permanently on that side of North America. Safe and secure harbors thus were to some a desideratum at least as important as anything in those areas like Texas where U.S. and Mexican interests seemed most immediately in conflict. San Francisco and Monterey Bays were directly across the broad Pacific from alluring Asian ports, and prevailing winds could hardly have been better positioned to carry traffic both ways. San Francisco, especially, inspired awe and ambition. Thomas Jefferson Farnham called it the "glory of the Western world," and Capt. Charles Wilkes thought it could hold all the navies of Europe at once. Wilkes's estimate implied a threat. If England should acquire San Francisco Bay, wrote the editor of the *American Review*, that nation would be "mistress of the seas … for all time" and, with Mexico as an ally, could choke off any future growth of the United States. Seen in this context, the Mexican War represented a vague but growing collective impulse toward the Pacific and beyond. Our former minister to Mexico wrote in 1842 that keeping England out of the Golden Gate would be worth a war of twenty years.[4]

Victory in the war, plus the gold rush, gave that impulse shape and substance and strengthened it as well. Wealth-seekers flocked to California from around the Pacific rim. This first phase of the rush, in fact, demonstrated that connections from California and Oregon to around the Pacific were far more natural than ones to the nation back east; travel time to San Francisco from Australia was about half that from New York City. Quickly, trade routes developed to places open to outsiders—early residents of the gold fields sent their dirty clothes to be laundered in Honolulu—and soon the pressure built to connect to places currently closed. It was no coincidence that Japan ended its isolation from the West only five years after the Mexican War, nor that the naval officer who opened the door was an American, Matthew Perry.

As with the contribution of far western resources to the rise of the new America, the implications of our nation's presence on the Pacific are easy to overlook exactly because they are so fundamental and so much a part of our present understanding of who we are. Our looking outward to Asia and our reception of peoples and influences from around the rim has resulted in a continuing tension between what we imagine as alluring possibilities and as grave dangers. Besides the apparently deathless dream of the China market and other economic aspirations, nineteenth-century commentators as diverse as Senator Thomas Hart Benton and John Cardinal Newman predicted the rise of a new super-civilization through the mingling of the finest flowerings of far-eastern cultures (usually meaning the Chinese) with the highest forms from the West (that is, us).[5] Others were just as enthusiastic with grim warnings about America being overrun by various Yellow Perils. The Chinese remain the only nationality in our history to be not merely discouraged in coming here but, in the Exclusion Act of 1884, to be explicitly forbidden.

All these fantasies, positive and negative, would prove way overblown, but our increasing integration into the Pacific world has been undeniable. The busiest U.S. port today is not New York or New Orleans but Los Angeles. The influence of Asian immigration—demographically, economically, intellectually, culturally—has been enormous and in recent years has only gathered momentum, especially in the western half of the nation. The human connections between our west coast and the Pacific world are ever more extensive. (A favorite bit of statistical trivia: Los Angeles exports more corpses than any port in the world as families send bodies of loved ones back to their birthplaces.) Our diplomatic tensions have followed a similar pattern. World War I would turn out to be our last war with a primarily Atlantic and European focus. Our involvement in the next one would begin and end in Asia, and the next two (and the one before, in the Philippines) were fought in Asia entirely. Looking back, the Mexican War began what we might ironically call the Pacification of America.

A third consequence of the Mexican War and far western expansion involves an unprecedented stimulus to the national infrastructure, what were called in the nineteenth century "internal improvements." The key point here was not what was in and on the land (that is, resources) or the land's location and geography (the Pacific coast and its ports) but the sheer size of what we acquired between 1845 and 1848. The influence was of space and distance. Although we had added an unprecedented amount of land to the nation, it was ours only on paper. The most pressing question was how it was to be truly integrated, starting with basic physical connections. The discovery of gold made that question immeasurably more pressing. The great coincidence of 1848 was in most ways very good news for the United States, but its immediate implication was extremely disturbing. On the one hand we had just acquired the most valuable land in the world. On the other hand that land was as far from the centers of national power and influence as was possible and still be inside the United States. Ports would open up oceanic connections between the west and east coasts, but clearly more direct, tighter, faster linkages were imperative.

What we needed, that is, was an expanded, even revolutionized system to move people, things and information around a far larger nation, especially between its eastern population and its glittering, distant and vulnerable western edge. As it happened, we had the technology for the job. Our defeat of Mexico coincided roughly with the first widespread use in the United States of the two most significant answers to the problem of distance: the railroad and the telegraph.

Although the first rail lines were built in the United States in the 1830s, railroad building got seriously underway only after the easing of a depression lasting from 1837 to 1841. The nation had about three thousand miles of track in 1841, more than five thousand in 1847, more than ten thousand in 1851, and more than twenty-two thousand in 1856. Virtually all of that was east of the Mississippi (there was one short line in California) but by then many were promoting railroads as the obvious way to bridge the distance to the Pacific coast. Three possible routes to the Pacific were surveyed, but opposition of southern politicians blocked any serious consideration of building a transcontinental line.

The Civil War opened the way, first by the withdrawal of southern opponents and second by sharpening the concern about tying California more closely to the Union in a time of crisis. Here was one way the Mexican and Civil Wars joined to shape the new America, in this case by providing the need and occasion for what at the time was the longest rail line in the world, the nation's most ambitious publicly funded project, and the grandest feat of engineering in modern history.

The modern telegraph similarly came into its own simultaneously with our acquiring the far West. Its first formal test, by Samuel F. B. Morse and Alfred Vail in May of 1844, came just six months before the election of the expansionist James K. Polk as president, less than a year before Texas was invited into the Union, barely two years before the start of the Mexican War, and fewer than four years before the United States acquired the Mexican Cession. Like the railroad, it first spread across the eastern third of the country, a copper web especially dense in the Northeast and Ohio

River valley. The telegraph was the most revolutionary development in the history of human communication. With minor exceptions like semaphore and carrier pigeons, it was the first time that information could move faster than people—and it was *so* much faster, virtually at the speed of light. It spread rapidly across Europe and much of Asia, then undersea cables allowed the connection of continents. By the mid-1870s New York (and thus hundreds of small American towns) was in direct touch with Tokyo.

As with the railroad, all this made the telegraph a natural step toward integrating the West into the nation, in this case through communication. And once again it was the Civil War that made it happen. Fears of Confederate influence encouraged congressional support of construction of a transcontinental telegraph line that began on July 4, 1861, the day Abraham Lincoln called up his first draft. The government contract called for completion within thirteen months. Astoundingly, the job was done by the end of October, nine months early. In the first message, California's chief justice assured President Lincoln of his state's loyalty to the Union.[6]

The problem of distance was also the problem of cost. No corporation, no matter how rich, would risk the money, even if it had it, to build a telegraph or rail line across the continent, especially since most of the country in the middle was empty of anyone who would pay to use either one. In both cases the answer was financial backing by the federal government. There was a close parallel between the two arrangements. The government loaned the Union and Central Pacific Railroads millions of dollars and gave them public land to sell; to build the telegraph it donated right of way and land for stations and guaranteed a minimum income after completion. The parallel between constructions was stunning. The Union Pacific built westward out of Omaha; so did the Western Union Company. The Central Pacific built eastward out of northern California; so did a partnership among California telegraph companies. Each railroad corporation created its own dummy construction company (the infamous Credit Mobilier for the Union Pacific), in effect hiring themselves, at inflated rates, to do the work; the two telegraph corporations did the same. Railroads and telegraphs both linked up in Utah near the Great Salt Lake.

So striking are the similarities, and so remarkable are the accomplishments, that it is easy to overlook a larger point. The twin constructions of the transcontinental telegraph and railroad came about through a new relationship between the central government and business, a marriage that provided public funds and security to corporate enterprise as a means to meet an unprecedented challenge. Similar arrangements, albeit no one of them on this scale, were forged by the federal government to meet the unprecedented needs of waging the Civil War. The war also, of course, compelled the government to consolidate and streamline its transportation and communication systems east of the Mississippi. Early in the fighting Oliver Wendell Holmes wrote that the telegraphic network was a "network of iron nerves which flash sensation and volition backward and forward to and from towns and provinces as if they were organs and limbs of a single living body." Railroads, in turn, were "a vast system of iron muscles which ... move the limbs of the mighty organism one upon another."[7] Together those systems, and the partnered forces of Civil War and westward expansion, served to consolidate a new nation.

The government-corporate relationships pioneered through western railroads and telegraphs and through new wartime arrangements became an increasingly integral part of the new America's economy. The variations in the far West were particularly effective in developing—some would say exploiting and often debauching—the resources discussed above. They began in the latter nineteenth century roughly coincident with building the transcontinentals. In the Mining Act of 1872, for instance,

Congress in effect gave the industry gargantuan subsidies by selling even the richest mining sites at a pittance—five dollars, half a sawbuck, per acre.[8] The government provided ranchers free grazing on public land and later leased the public domain at low rates. In the twentieth century the nearly infinite elaborations of such partnerships have been woven throughout the economy—a modern fact of life that arose from two crises, knitting a vast new West into the Union and keeping that expanded Union from splitting apart. Those crises in turn were associated with the nineteenth century's two transforming conflicts, the Mexican and Civil Wars.

In one other subtler way the two wars came together with new technologies, a new relationship between government and business, and new resources to shape the new American state. The first transcontinental railroad was officially completed on May 10, 1869. At its famous culmination at Promontory Summit, Leland Stanford swung a sledge to hammer the final spike into its pre-drilled hole. Wires were attached to sledge and spike so that when the blow was struck a circuit would be closed, which in turn would send a single electrical impulse across the national telegraphic grid that had been cleared of traffic for the occasion. That one impulse, in Morse code a momentous dot, marked the bridging of the continent. Far less publicized was another celebratory instant on San Francisco Bay, the grandest of those recently acquired ports looking outward toward Pacific possibilities. An enterprising officer had connected the nearest telegraphic receiver to the firing mechanism of a fifteen-inch artillery piece he had aimed across the bay. At the millisecond Stanford's hammer touched the spike, an artillery shot was launched westward through the Golden Gate.

I doubt any poet could imagine a more fitting image for the new America's sense of blossoming power and destiny for the coming century. Its distances spanned, its riches being tapped, time itself overcome by instant communication, its sprawling spaces drawn into national control, the United States now might look outward toward new conquests. There was something about the two events—the Civil War, confirming the Union and invigorating the national government, and far western expansion, enriching the nation and demonstrating its potentials—that combined to feed the new state's imperial tendencies. Certainly the two worked together to subdue resistance to national authority inside the acquired lands. Virtually all officers of the western army after 1865 were Civil War veterans who turned their experience in fighting Confederates to corralling and defeating Indians, and in the effort they relied on the new government-funded systems provoked by the challenges of mastering western conditions. The railroad and telegraph gave the army a mobility and an informational network that undercut what few advantages its Indian opponents had.

That connection between the Civil War, western growth and empire in turn should remind us of a fourth and final consequence of the Mexican War in shaping the modern American state. The war, with the addition of Texas and the Pacific Northwest, triggered a racial crisis. Writing that will surprise few if any readers, but the crisis I mean was broader and more complex than as it has been almost always described, and its influence on our history has been far more complicated and ambiguous.

Every textbook of American history considers in some detail how the Mexican War raised, once and for all as it turned out, the explosive question of whether African-American slavery would be allowed into western federal lands. Politicians had hoped that question had been closed for good by the Missouri Compromise of 1820-21, which divided western lands not yet organized as states along a line at thirty-six degrees, thirty minutes (the southern boundary of Missouri). All federal lands south of that line (Arkansas and Indian Territory) would be open to slavery; everything north (what is today Kansas, Nebraska, the Dakotas and the Montana and Wyoming plains) would not. Presumably that would mean that any states organized from those two areas would enter the Union as slave and non-slave states, respectively. At the time of that arrangement, however, the United States stopped at the Texas border to the south and at the continental divide to the West. The compromise would not apply to any new lands added to the nation. Texas, with its thousands of bondsmen, was admitted not as a federal territory but as a slave state, so it did not re-open the question. But the Pacific Northwest and the Mexican Cession would be federally administered lands, public domain. Some southern slaves were there but nothing close to a critical mass. The new lands—especially the Mexican Cession, since the Southwest presumably would receive many immigrants out of the South— tossed into the political arena the issue of "free soil," whether or not the federal government would permit slaveowners to take their human property into the new territories.

This made the Mexican War, in Ralph Waldo Emerson's phrase, a "dose of arsenic" poisoning the body politic. The fighting had barely begun when debates over the expansion of slavery began raging in Congress. The Compromise of 1850 failed to truly face the issue, then the Kansas-Nebraska Act of 1854 brought it again to the fore by effectively nullifying the Missouri Compromise. The free soil struggle in Kansas saw the first shedding of blood over the question, and in retrospect the slide toward disunion was rapid and, if not inevitable, at least one of awful momentum.

That racial crisis—the one over the deeply rooted institution of black slavery and its place in the new country and in national life— is a standard part of any survey of American history. But it was only half the story. Acquiring the far West precipitated another crisis. It literally came with the territory. To appreciate it, we have to move beyond what for too long has been a tendency to think of race in American history in terms of black and white, African Americans and everybody else. American race, and ethnicity, have always involved much more than that. Certainly at the time considered here the term "race" was applied across the ethnic spectrum. Groups as diverse as Chinese, American Indians and even Irish and Italians were referred to as races.[9]

If we use the loose definition of race of the time, acquiring more than a million square miles between 1845 and 1848 complicated hugely the nation's racial makeup. Consider one crude measure. While the land size of the United States increased by about two thirds, the estimated number of languages spoken in the nation doubled, considering the dozens of Native American peoples suddenly inside our borders. Then came the gold rush and a flood of persons from around the Pacific rim and then from Europe and much of the rest of the world. By 1850 California was likely the most polyglot place of its size on earth.

Most of those new peoples brought suddenly into the Union, furthermore, had never had more than the slightest contact with the nation, its people and its institutions. Hispanic peoples of the Southwest were the closest, but they lived under a far-northern variant of Spanish culture, a hybrid heavily influenced by Native Americans. Native Americans themselves, apart from the fur trade, for the most part had not played the slightest role in the nation's economic life. Most who called the West home in 1848, that is, were essentially outsiders—culturally, economically, socially, religiously. The gold rush immediately brought other outsiders, more Spanish-speaking immigrants from South America and exotics such as Hawaiians (also called Kanakans). Next, after 1852, California and the West received tens of thousands of the most culturally anomalous immigrants in American history, the Chinese.[10]

All this raised troubling questions. Could these various peoples, brought suddenly inside the nation's borders, be integrated into American life? And if they could, how and on what terms? And if they couldn't, what was to be done with them? It was the human equivalent to the challenge of tying the vast new territories physically into the nation. The government was meeting that geographical challenge by building transcontinental railroads and telegraphs and by forging an unprecedented relationship between itself and new concentrations of corporate wealth. The answer to the racial question was more elusive. An earlier response, in the case of Indian peoples to the east, had been to remove them farther west. The idea was that, instead of integrating them right away into American society, they could be pushed beyond its nether edge and hopefully transformed. The great expansion, however, took us to that magnificent, port-poor Pacific coast. Short of putting tens of thousands of persons on barges anchored west of San Francisco and Los Angeles, removal to the west was not an option.

So the great expansion triggered two racial crises.[11] The one most remembered involved African Americans, racial insiders locked with white Americans in an awful and intimate embrace for more than two centuries. This crisis raised the question of whether the system that enslaved these racial insiders would be allowed in the new lands as the West's rich, varied resources began to be put to national purposes. Beyond that, it asked the question of whether the West would be open to any blacks at all, slave or free. After Oregon Territory's legislature voted to forbid slavery, it immediately added a provision outlawing the immigration of free blacks. These questions, especially on the expansion of slavery, lit the fuse of Civil War.

The second crisis raised the question of what place, if any, there was in the expanded Union for peoples already living in new lands, including many who had called them home for thousands of years. This question, too, had violent possibilities. The gold rush offered a grim example. When the forty-niners arrived in the gold fields, they found many of the richest diggings already being worked by persons living in California at the time of the discovery or arrived there from around the Pacific rim. These forty-*eighters* were mostly racial outsiders—Peruvians and Chileans, Californios (Hispanic Californians), Hawaiians and local Indians. Most were soon expelled from the mines, often violently. Gold strikes were often on Indian homelands. That, plus the inevitable tensions arising when hordes of newcomers disrupted native economies, led to some of the most appalling atrocities in North American history— organized hunts to exterminate Indians, enslavement of Indians of both sexes and rapes of Indian women, the theft and sale of Indian children. The worst assaults happened during the 1850s. That was the decade of Bleeding Kansas, and although the toll in deaths was quite likely at least a hundred times as great, in our textbooks the California bloodshed and the broader tensions behind it rarely get even a sentence.[12]

This violence made the Mexican War profoundly ironic. The word "racist" is tossed around far too easily by some in describing American foreign policy (and American policies generally), but for our war with Mexico, it's on the mark. The conflict was justified as the rightful expansion of a superior Anglo civilization over darker peoples who were stunted in culture, incapable of using the land as God meant, and unlikely to pose much resistance to American conquest. Popular literature of the day was full of images of "Mexican monkeys" and slobbering savages. Many predicted that these lesser peoples would somehow melt away before the vigorous advance of white America.

But of course they did not evaporate. They remained, and soon their lands were being brought within the nation, not just on paper but in fact, and more quickly than anyone had anticipated. That in turn left us with a dicey issue. Those peoples living in the far West at the time it was conquered, the ones so recently dismissed as alien and inferior—how would they fit into American life?

Seen together, the two racial crises and the Mexican and Civil Wars had at least one thing in common—they forced and complicated the issue of citizenship. The Mexican War pressed on those who already had it the question of whether citizenship could and should be extended to peoples who differed considerably in their life ways and cultural norms—in how they used and thought about the land, how they supported themselves, how they worshiped and conversed and conceived of their families. The Civil War destroyed African-American slavery and opened the way, soon taken, to expanding citizenship to include freed slaves. But by doing that, of course, the two wars and their aftermaths only opened a slew of other questions about racial outsiders and insiders—and therefore about everybody else. What did being a citizen entail? What were the obligations of governments— federal, state and local—in defining the rights and demands of citizenship and in protecting the one and in making sure the other was met? The case of far western Indian peoples raised especially nettlesome questions. While African Americans had clamored for citizenship, and in many cases had died fighting for it, many Indians wished to stay as they were, figuratively outside the national house, both in their allegiance and ways of life. How far should the government go in imposing citizenship? In forcing people to conform to a cultural checklist that now defined what a citizen was and how one behaved?

In the abstract similar questions had been asked since the revolution and before. The Mexican and Civil Wars, however, made those questions real. By bringing so many culturally anomalous peoples inside the nation's borders and by liberating four million slaves, they opened the possibility of a far wider citizenship, specifically one far more racially and culturally complicated. Neither war began with that in mind, but that's what they did: forced Americans to ask whether they were willing to live much more fully into the American Revolution's implied promise. Together the conflicts might be called the Wars of Put Up or Shut Up.

Ultimately we Put Up, at least more so than not. Along the way, of course, there was plenty of resistance, plenty who considered Indians and Hispanics and African Americans no more fit for citizenship than giraffes or hedgehogs. Besides that, Putting Up turned out to mean pushing citizenship on those who didn't want it, most obviously many Indian peoples, and fighting more wars to bless them with its benefits. Some, like George Custer, survived the war that opened the door for those longing to walk through it, only to die trying to drag in others who wanted to stay outside. The 20 years after 1845, that is, introduced the enduring puzzles around racial and ethnic minorities in national life, the messy and contentious questions that have so enlivened politics in the new American state.

Even more broadly, the two wars raised issues about the nature of the nation itself. That term, "nation," usually had meant a collection of persons related by blood and deep-rooted traditions. Its sense had been rather close to that of a tribe writ large. During the late nineteenth century two new nations appeared, half a world apart, each finding its identity in that traditional idea—Japan, blending a commitment to modernization with its very old view of itself as an island people kin-bound and dedicated to divine monarchy, and Germany, binding together its several states through a sense of collective character and blood ties summed up in *volk*. The United States meanwhile was moving decisively in another direction. Among the many ways this country might be understood, one is as an ongoing audacious experiment in a radically different definition of nationhood—not a union of blood and tradition but a collective commitment to institutions and ideals, to "the notion," as Alan Trachtenberg recently put it, "of a civil realm of laws, rights, and citizenship," regardless of the participants' genealogy and traditions.[13] From day one that new definition met resistance and raised devilish problems, but the changes brought on by the Mexican and Civil Wars would test that experiment far more rigorously than ever. Soon other developments in the new American state, notably the surge of "new immigration" from eastern and southern Europe, would add their own stresses and challenges.

The political and cultural life of twentieth century America has been shaped significantly by the tussling over our distinctive approach to nationhood and by issues sharpened by events between 1845 and 1865. The eugenics movement and the second Ku Klux Klan and efforts to limit and channel immigration in the 1920s, Americanization movements, the ethnic and racial crosscurrents of the New Deal, including its programs to restore and cultivate Indian cultures, the civil rights movement (defined broadly to include Native American rights and Hispanic-based issues such as migrant labor), the recent contentions over cultural and racial diversity and certainly the current dust-ups over the new-new immigration and recent dire alarms about new Yellow and Brown Perils—they all have had various beginnings, but the questions around them all were brought to the fore by the twinned racial crises after 1848 and by the Wars of Put Up or Shut Up.

Those questions, to say the least, are still with us. Their emotional volatility is high and their flashpoints low, as shown in the heat generated by seemingly tame issues like bilingual public education. The broader promises of citizenship, especially a fuller participation in the American material dream, remain elusive. In the rankings for the dubious distinction of the nation's poorest counties, the top spots almost always are held by places dominated by groups invited into political life in the great expansion and the Civil War, counties in the Mississippi Delta, along the Texas-Mexico border, and around Indian reservations.

The enduring conflicts and frustrations are as much a part of the modern American state as the other fruits of the Mexican War—a vast national domain, resources that have transformed the nation and have gone a long way toward making it the most powerful in history, sophisticated systems of movement and communication built by partnerships of governments and corporations, an increasingly westward-tilting, Pacific-facing perspective and a confident (some would say swaggering) presence in a larger world, especially that to the west and south of what we added in the great expansion.

Endnotes

From Murfreesboro to Buena Vista
By Donald S. Frazier

1 Matt Riddick to Augustus Valerius Ball, Shelbyville, Tenn., Feb. 11, 1863, transcription in possession of the author, original letter in the private collection of Anne Ryals, Montgomery, Alabama.

Window on the Southwest:
Arkansas's Role in the Mexican War
By C. Fred Williams

1 For general histories of Arkansas prior to Mexican War see S. Charles Bolton, *Remote and Restless: Arkansas 1800-1860* (Fayetteville: University of Arkansas Press, 1998); Ed Bearss and Arrell M. Gibson, *Fort Smith: Little Gibraltar on the Arkansas* (Norman: University of Oklahoma Press, 1969), and Lonnie J. White, *Politics on the Southwestern Frontier: Arkansas Territory, 1819-1836* (Memphis: Memphis State University Press, 1964).

2 An Act establishing a separate territorial government in the southern part of the territory of Missouri. (a) Be it enacted by the Senate and House of Representatives of the United States of America, in Congress assembled, That from and after the fourth day of July next, all that part of the territory of Missouri which lies South of a line, beginning on the Mississippi river, at thirty six degrees, north latitude, running thence west to the river St. Francois; thence, up the same, to thirty six degrees thirty minutes north latitude ; and thence, west to the western territorial boundary line; shall, for the purposes of a territorial government, constitute a separate territory, and be called the Arkansaw territory ... *Statutes at Large*: Fifteenth Congress Sess. II, CH 40 1819, 493-4.

3 For a general history of the Florida question see Leitch Wright, Jr., *Anglo-Spanish Rivalry in North America* (Athens: University of Georgia Press, 1971). Old but still useful Isaac J. Cox, *The West Florida Controversy* (Baltimore: Johns Hopkins Press, 1918). For the Texas question see David M. Vignes, *The Revolutionary Decades: The Saga of Texas, 1810-1836* (Austin: University of Texas Press, 1965) and Seymour v. Connor, *Adventure in Glory: The Saga of Texas, 1836-1849* (Austin: University of Texas Press, 1965).

4 William Earl Weeks *John Quincy Adams and American Global Empire* (Lexington: University of Kentucky Press, 1992), 72-75.

5 Ibid., 76-79.

6 Ibid., 106-109 and Robert V. Remini, *Andrew Jackson and the Course of American Empire, 1767-1821* (New York: Harper & Collins, 1977), 301-05; 324-25; 344-45.

7 Weeks, *John Quincy Adams and Global Empire*, 119-124; 136-37; 162-68.

8 Bolton, *Remote and Restless*, 10-11; 24-26.

9 Eugene C. Baker, *Mexico and Texas, 1821-1835* (Austin: University of Texas Press, 1928) and White, *Politics on the Southwestern Frontier*, 48-52.

10 Thomas D. Clark and John D. W. Guice, *Frontiers in Conflict: The Old Southwest, 1795-17830* (Albuquerque: University of New Mexico Press, 1989).

11 Bolton, *Remote and Restless*, 67-88.

12 Bearss and Gibson, *Fort Smith: Little Gibraltar on the Arkansas*,8-19.

13 W. David Baird, "Arkansas's Choctaw Boundary: A Case of Justice Delayed," *Arkansas Historical Quarterly 28* (Autumn, 1969): 203-22.

14 *Arkansas Gazette*, March 3, 1825.

15 Baird, "Arkansas's Choctaw Boundary," 210-15.

16 An Act to fix the western boundary line of the territory of Arkansas, and or other purposes. (a) Be it enacted by the Senate and House of Representatives of the United States of America, in Congress assembled, That the western boundary line of the territory of Arkansas shall begin at a point forty miles west of the south-west corner of the state of Missouri, and run south to the right bank of the Red River, and thence, down the river, and with the Mexican boundary, to the line of the state of Louisiana, any law heretofore made to the contrary notwithstanding ... *Statutes at Large*: Eighteenth Congress Sess. I, CH 155 May 26, 1824, 40.

17 ART. 1. The Western boundary of Arkansas shall be, and the same is, hereby defined, *viz*: A line shall be run, commencing on Red River, at the point where the Eastern Choctaw line strikes said River, and run due North with said line to the River Arkansas, thence in a direct line to the South West corner of Missouri ... May 6, 1828. *Indian Affairs: Laws and Treaties*. Vol. II (Treaties) in part. Compiled and edited by Charles J. Kappler. (Washington: Government Printing Office, 1904), 288.

18 The Indian country west of the Mississippi river, that is bounded north by the north line of lands assigned to the Osage tribe of Indians, produced east to the state of Missouri: west, by the Mexican possessions; south, by Red river; and east, by the west line of the territory of Arkansas and the state of Missouri, ... *Indian Intercourse Act, 1834*.

19 Robert Paul Markman, "The Arkansas Cherokees, 1817-1828," (Ph.D. Dissertation, University of Oklahoma, 1972).

20 Ronald N. Satz, *American Indian Policy in the Jacksonian Era* (Lincoln: University of Nebraska Press, 1975), 220-22.

21 Lonnie White, "Disturbances on the Arkansas Texas Boarder, 1817-1831," *Arkansas Historical Quarterly*, 19 (Summer, 1960): 95-110.

22 Harold W. Ryan, "Matthew Arbuckle Comes to Fort Smith," *Arkansas Historical Quarterly*. 19 (Winter, 1960): 287-92.

23 Boyd Johnson, *The Arkansas Frontier* (Little Rock: Privately Printed, 1957), 101-03.

24 *Arkansas Gazette*, March 25, 1834.

25 Ira Don Richards, *Story of a Rivertown: Little Rock in the Nineteenth Century* (Benton: Privately Printed, 1969), 32-33.

26 *Statutes at Large*: Twenty-third Congress Sess. I, CH 161 1834, 733.

27 Dewy Stokes, "Public Affairs in Arkansas, 1830-1850," (Ph.D. Dissertation, University of Texas, 1968). 75-78.

28 Louise Berry, "The Fort Leavenworth-Fort Gibson Military Road the Founding of Fort Scott," *Kansas Historical Quarterly*, 11 (May, 1942), 1-19.

29 Bearss and Gibson, *Fort Smith: Little Gibraltar on the Arkansas*, 142-43.

30 Ibid., 143.

31 Ibid.

32 Ibid., 144.

33 *Laws of the United States, op. cit.*, p. 337. A memorial dated October 23, 1833, from the general assembly of the territory of Arkansas, asking the removal of Fort Gibson to the old site of Fort Smith (on the Arkansas boundary), was communicated to the house January 13, 1834. In 1825, by congressional act, the boundary of Arkansas was moved forty miles west of its present location. Fort Smith, on the old boundary, was abandoned and Fort Gibson (established in 1824) protected the new frontier.
Few recognized the U.S.'s vulnerability on the frontier better than Arkansans. Led by Senator Ambrose Sevier, the state's congressional delegation that included Senator William Fulton and Congressman Archibald Yell, kept the Indian issue before Jackson and his successor Martin Van Buren. Sevier came to believe that Congress erred in granting tribal autonomy over Indian vs. Indian crimes and urged his colleagues to pass new legislation that would allow U.S. courts to have jurisdiction over certain cases. However, he failed to convince enough of the lawmakers to make that happen.

34 Congress responded May 14, 1836, appropriating $50,000 for the removal of Fort Gibson to a location "on or near the western frontier line of Arkansas." In 1838 the forty-mile strip was ceded by the government to the Cherokee Indians and the Arkansas boundary fixed again at the old location. Fort Gibson remained in the Cherokee country.

35 Bearss and Gibson, *Fort Smith: Little Gibraltar on the Arkansas*. 146-48.

36 Grant Foreman, *Advancing the Frontier, 1830-1860* (Norman: University of Oklahoma Press, 1933), 324-28.

37 Satz, *American Indian Policy in the Jacksonian Era*, 221-22.

38 Richard L Trotter, "For the Defense of the Western Border: Arkansas Volunteers on the Indian Frontier, 1846-1847," *Arkansas Historical Quarterly* 60 (Winter 2001): 394-410.

39 Ibid.

40 Ibid.

Rackensack in the Field:
Arkansans in the U.S.-Mexican War
By William A. Frazier

1 *Arkansas Gazette*, June 15, 1846. A reading of the Arkansas newspapers of June and July, 1846, offers several references to the hopes of bringing honor and glory to the young state in the war. The *Banner* and the *Democrat* are the two other Little Rock papers, the latter of which was edited at the time by former *Gazette* editor William Woodruff. Other Arkansas newspapers of the era, all weeklies, referenced cited herein include Van Buren's *Arkansas Intelligencer* and the *Washington Telegraph*. They will be cited without the "Arkansas."

2 Desmond Walls Allen, *Arkansas' Mexican War Soldiers* (Conway: Arkansas Research, 1988), 1-4, 91; *Democrat*, April 16, August 13, 1847; *Gazette*, May 8, June 5, 1847. Jonathan H. Buhoup, *Narrative of the Central Division or Army of Chihuahua, Commanded by Brigadier General Wool* (Pittsburgh: M.P. Morse, 1847), 137; Maurice Garland Fulton, ed., *Diary and Letters of Josiah Gregg, Southwestern Enterprises, 1840-1847, Volume II* (Norman: University of Oklahoma Press, 1941), 67-68. In Allen, the infantry battalion lists Captain Stephen Enyart's men as a company of one hundred men. Enyart's reconstitution of the company in 1847 included infantrymen from the battalion recruited in 1846. In Meares's company, a portion of the re-enlistments were also composed of former Illinois infantry. Wood's company was recruited in Washington, Madison, Benton and Crawford counties. Anthony's Arkansans were recruited in Washington and Benton counties.

3 *Telegraph*, Sept. 2, 1846; *Democrat*, July 10, Aug. 5, August 28, 1846; *Gazette*, June 8, 1846.

4 Allen, *Arkansas's Soldiers*, 2-3.

5 *Gazette*, June 5, 1846

6 *Gazette*, April 13, July 13, Aug. 24, 1846; *Democrat*, June 26, 1846; Allen, *Arkansas's Soldiers*, 2-7; David Y. Thomas, *Arkansas and Its People, A History 1541-1930* 1 (New York: The American Historical Society, Inc., 1930), 105-07; ibid. 2, 825; Fay Hempstead, *Pictorial History of Arkansas* (St. Louis and New York, N. D. Thompson publishing company, 1890), 1204; William W. Hughes, *Archibald Yell* (Fayetteville: The University of Arkansas Press, 1988), 19-22, 28-29, 47-48; *Register of the Officers and Cadets of the U.S. Military Academy*, (West Point: New York, 1939, 1840); *Engineer Department Letters Received Relating to the U.S. Military Academy, 1819-1866* (West Point Military Academy), National Archives, Microfilm Publication M2047. An advertisement in the April 13, 1846, *Gazette* shows a man named Meares as an attorney in Lafayette County, which other records indicate was Meares's home at the time.

7 *Democrat*, June 26, 1846; *Gazette*, July 20, 1846; Hughes, *Archibald Yell*, 103; Robert Walter Johannsen, *To The Halls of the Montezumas; The Mexican War in the American Imagination* (New York: Oxford University Press, 1985), 121; George Winston Smith and Charles Judah, *Chronicles of the Gringos: The U.S.*

Army in the Mexican War, 1846-1848 (Albuquerque: The University of New Mexico Press, 1968), 468; Justin H. Smith, *The War With Mexico* I, (New York: The Macmillan Company, 1919), 269.

8 Samuel E. Chamberlain, *My Confession* (New York: Harper and Brothers, 1956), 65.

9 Buhoup, *Narrative*, 15.

10 *Gazette*, Jan. 9, 1847.

11 Buhoup, *Narrative*, 35.

12 Buhoup, *Narrative*, 67-72.

13 Buhoup, *Narrative*, 30-33, 40, 42-43,50; John C. Palmer Diary, Henry E. Huntington Library and Art Gallery, San Marino, Calif., 34, 45, 54; Jacob Medart Smith Diary, Henry E. Huntington Library and Art Gallery; Dec. 27, 1847.

14 Buhoup, *Narrative*, 47-48

15 *Gazette*, January 23, 27, 1847; Buhoup, *Narrative*, 88-91; Fulton, *Gregg* I, 292, 294.

16 *Telegraph*, Sept. 2, 1846; *Democrat*, July 10, Aug. 5, Aug. 28, 1846.

17 *Democrat*, Jan. 1, 1847; *Gazette*, Oct. 26, 1846. It is worth noting that Yell and Borland were quarreling at this time and the separation of the two may have also had some bearing.

18 *Gazette*, Jan. 23, Feb. 13, 1847; *Democrat*, Jan. 29, 1847.

19 *Gazette*, Aug. 24, 1846.

20 *Democrat*, Dec. 10, Dec. 17, 1847

21 *Democrat*, July 20, 1847, Feb. 18, 1848; *Intelligencer*, April 24, Aug. 7, 1847; *Gazette*, Dec. 16, 1847.

22 *Gazette*, Feb. 6, Feb. 13, 1847; Chamberlain, *My Confession*, 83.

23 Palmer Diary, 61-62; *Banner*, Feb. 17, 1847

24 *Gazette*, Feb. 27, March 20, 1847, *Banner*, March 24, 1847;

25 Buhoup, *Narrative*, 106.

26 Buhoup, *Narrative*, 106; Fulton, *Gregg* II, 36-37; Heitman, *Army Register*, 48; Otto B. Engelman, trans., "The Second Illinois in the Mexican War: Mexican War Letters of Adolphus Engelman, 1846-1847," *Journal of the Illinois State Historical Society* 26 (January 1934): 440; *Gazette*, July 22, 1847.

27 Chamberlain, *My Confession*, 87-88; Palmer Diary, Feb. 13 entry.

28 Taylor to Yell, Feb. 14, 1847, Archibald Yell Letter Book, University of Arkansas at Little Rock, Ottenheimer Library, Manuscripts and Special Archives Department; ibid, Yell to Taylor, Feb. 19, 1847; *Gazette*, March 27, 1847.

29 General Zachary Taylor's Orders, Mexican War, General Orders, No. 24, No. 30; Buhoup, *Narrative*, 134-35.

30 John S.D. Eisenhower, *So Far From God, The U.S. War with Mexico, 1846-1848* (New York: Doubleday, 1989), 72; Thomas Bangs Thorpe, *Our Army on the Rio Grande* (Philadelphia: Carey and Hart, 1846), 66, 105.

31 Walter Lee Brown, *A Life of Albert Pike* (Fayetteville: The University of Arkansas Press, 1997), 126-27, 149; *Gazette*, May 25, 1846; *Democrat*, June 12, 1846.

32 Eisenhower, *So Far From God*, 84. The city that grew up around the fort is modern-day Brownsville.

33 *Register of the Officers and Cadets of the U.S. Military Academy* (West Point: New York, 1844), n.p.

34 James Henry Carleton, *The Battle of Buena Vista with Operations of the Army of Occupation for One Month* (New York: Harper and Brothers, 1848), 212.

35 Eisenhower, *So Far From God*, 183.

36 Buhoup, *Narrative*, 109.

37 *Battle of Buena Vista*, 24-25.

38 Buhoup, *Narrative*, 109.

39 Eisenhower, *So Far From God*, 182.

40 Palmer Diary, 87. Pike's squadron had been stationed at Palomas Pass, away from the rest of the Arkansas Regiment, while constructing a defensive position. It was abandoned before the Mexican troops arrived.

41 Buhoup, *Narrative*, 113.

42 Robert Selph Henry, *The Story of the Mexican War* (Indianapolis: The Bobbs-Merrill Company, Inc., 1950), 247.

43 Carleton, *Battle of Buena Vista*, 31.

44 K. Jack Bauer, *Zachary Taylor, Soldier Planter Statesman of the Old Southwest* (Baton Rouge: Louisiana State University Press, 1985), 193.

45 George Winston Smith and Charles Judah, *Chronicles of the Gringos: The U.S. Army in the Mexican War, 1846-1848* (Albuquerque: The University of New Mexico Press, 1968), 100-103; Eisenhower, *So Far From God*, 186-187.

46 *Gazette*, April 17, 1847.

47 Carleton, *Battle of Buena Vista*, 39-42.

48 Ibid., 47.

49 Buhoup, *Narrative*, 117-18.

50 Carleton, *Battle of Buena Vista*, 48-49.

51 Buhoup, *Narrative*, 120-21.

52 Fulton, *Gregg* II , 71; Francis Baylies, *Narrative of Major General Wool's Campaign in Mexico* (Albany: Little & Company, 1851), 37; Buhoup, *Narrative*, 123-125.

53 Eisenhower, *So Far From God*, 188-190.

54 *Gazette*, April 17, 1847.

55 Buhoup, *Narrative*, 123-125.

56 *Democrat*, April 16, 1847.

57 *The Picket Guard*, May 17, 1847 (newspaper printed at Saltillo by Illinois volunteers).

58 Carleton, *The Battle of Buena Vista*, 212.

59 Chamberlain, *My Confession, Recollections of a Rogue* edited by William H. Goetzmann (Austin: Texas State Historical Association, 1996), 172. This later version of the Chamberlain memoir includes an illustration of the Arkansas flags draped over O'Brien's captured cannons after the battle of Buena Vista.

60 *Gazette*, April 17, 1847.

61 Buhoup, *Narrative*, 129.

62 Smith and Judah, *Chronicles of the Gringos*, 343-45.

63 Fulton, *Gregg* II, 65.

64 Carleton, *Battle of Buena Vista*, 129-33; Buhoup, *Narrative*, 132.

65 Smith, *The War with Mexico II*, 25-26.

66 Theophilus F. Rodenbough and William L. Haskin, eds., *The Army of the United States, Historical Sketches of Staff and Line with Portraits of Generals-in-Chief* (New York: Maynard, Merrill, and Co., 1896), 195

67 *Banner*, June 9, 1847.

68 *Democrat*, Aug. 13, Dec. 10, 1847

69 Robert Selph Henry, *The Story of the Mexican War* (New York: Frederick Ungar Publishing Co., 1961), 327; Gustavus Woodson Smith, *Company "A" Corps of Engineers, U.S.A., 1846-1848, in the Mexican War*, ed. Leonne M. Hudson (Kent, Ohio: Kent State University Press: 2001), 47.; Bauer, *The Mexican War*, 292-94.

70 *Democrat*, Dec. 17, 1847.

71 *Democrat*, Oct. 22, 1847; New Orleans *Times Picayune*, Sept. 9, 1847.

72 *Democrat*, Dec. 17, 1847.

73 *Democrat*, Oct. 22, Dec. 3, Dec. 17, 1847, Feb. 18, 1848.

74 Henry, *Story of the Mexican War*, 386-391; David M. Pletcher, *The Diplomacy of Annexation* (Columbia: University of Missouri Press, 1973), 562-64; Bauer, *The Mexican War*, 388.

75 William F. Pope, *Early Days in Arkansas, Being for the Most Part the Personal Recollections of an Old Settler* (Little Rock: Frederick W. Allsopp, 1895), 277-78.

76 *Democrat*, April 16, 1847.

The View from the Other Side: Mexican Historiographical Perspectives on the 1846-1848 War With the United States
By Pedro Santoni

1 Lynnell Hancock (with Nina Biddle and Pat Wingert), "History Lessons," *Newsweek*, July 10, 1995.

2 Otis A. Singletary, *The Mexican War* (Chicago: The University of Chicago Press, 1960), 4-5. The quoted words appear in Robert W. Johannsen, *To the Halls of the Montezumas: The Mexican War in the American Imagination* (New York: Oxford University Press, 1985), vii.

3 Tim Weiner, "Of Gringos and Old Grudges: This Land is Their Land," *The New York Times*, Jan. 9, 2004.

4 Michael C. Meyer, William L. Sherman, and Susan M. Deeds, *The Course of Mexican History*, 7th ed. (New York: Oxford University Press, 2003), 335.

5 Grant Wahl, "Yes, Hard Feelings," *Sports Illustrated*, March 28, 2005.

6 Alvaro Matute, "Conciencia histórica temprana. Cuatro ejemplos," in *México en guerra (1846-1848): Perspectivas regionales*, Laura Herrera Serna, coord. (Mexico City: Consejo Nacional para la Cultura y las Artes, 1997), 54.

7 Richard Griswold del Castillo, *The Treaty of Guadalupe Hidalgo: A Legacy of Conflict* (Norman: University of Oklahoma Press, 1990), 114.

8 Gene M. Brack, *Mexico Views Manifest Destiny, 1821-1846: An Essay on the Origins of the Mexican War* (Albuquerque: University of New Mexico Press, 1975), 25.

9 Historians still debate whether or not Otero authored the pamphlet. Jesús Reyes Heroles has made the case for Otero's authorship, but others, like Andrés Lira, point instead to a collective effort. For more on the dispute, see Matute, "Conciencia histórica," 48-49.

10 [Mariano Otero], *Consideraciones sobre la situación política y social de la república mexicana en el año de 1847* (Mexico City: Valdés y Redondas, 1848), 13-16, 18, 22, and 24.

11 [Otero], *Consideraciones*, 31, 35, 37, 40, and 42.

12 Matute, "Conciencia histórica," 48.

13 Griswold del Castillo, *The Treaty*, 116.

14 José Fernando Ramírez, *Mexico During the War with the United States*, Walter B. Scholes, ed., Elliot B. Scherr, trans. (Columbia, Mo.: University of Missouri Press, 1950), 14.

15 Michael P. Costeloe, *The Central Republic in Mexico, 1835-1846: Hombres de Bien in the Age of Santa Anna* (New York: Cambridge University Press, 1993), 261, 267-268.

16 Ramírez, *Mexico During the War*, 14, 30, 41-42. The only biographical study of Gómez Pedraza is Laura Solares Robles, *Una revolución pacífica: Biografía política de Manuel Gómez Pedraza, 1789-1851* (Mexico City: Instituto de Investigaciones José María Luis Mora, 1996).

17 To be fair, Ramírez did not spare other newspapers from fault. He commented that the *puro*-supported *La Voz del Pueblo* "helped the [Paredes'] revolution because it made the soldiers consider the [Herrera] government a constant threat to their existence and to their special privileges; it cut the army off from the society by urging it into open warfare against the people." Ramírez, *Mexico During the War*, 44.

18 All quotes in this paragraph come from Ramírez, *Mexico During the War*; the first appears in 82-83, the second in 71, and the third in 111.

19 Will Fowler, *Mexico in the Age of Proposals, 1821-1853* (Westport, Conn.: Greenwood Press, 1998), 101, 122, n. 3.; the quote is from Carlos María Bustamante, *El nuevo Bernal Díaz del Castillo, o sea, historia de la invasión de los anglo-americanos en México*, 2 vols. (Mexico City: Instituto Nacional de Estudios Históricos de la Revolución Mexicana, 1987 [reprint ed., 1847]), 1: 3.

20 Bustamante, *El nuevo Bernal*, 2: 89-92.

21 Bustamante, *El nuevo Bernal*, 2: 186.

22 Bustamante, *El nuevo Bernal*, 2: 130.

23 The text of the Santa Anna's first proclamation can be found in *Memoria de la primera secretaría de estado y del despacho de Relaciones Interiores y Exteriores de los Estados Unidos Mexicanos, leida al soberano Congreso constituyente en los días 14, 15 y 16 de diciembre de 1846, por el ministro del ramo José María Lafragua* (Mexico City: Imprenta de Vicente García Torres, 1847), app., 109-115; the second message, a Sept. 14, 1846 letter to José María Almonte, appeared in *El Republicano* (Mexico City), Sept. 16, 1846.

24 Bustamante, *El nuevo Bernal*, 2: 99.

25 Griswold del Castillo, *The Treaty*, 115.

26 Carmen Vázquez Mantecón, *Santa Anna y la encrucijada del Estado: La dictadura (1853-1855)* (Mexico City: Fondo de Cultura Económica, 1986), 107-108.

27 Vázquez Mantecón, *Santa Anna y la encrucijada*, 215; and Matute, "Conciencia histórica," 52. The quote is from Ramón Alcaraz, et.al., *The Other Side: or Notes for the History of the War Between Mexico and the United States*, Albert C. Ramsey, trans. (New York: Burt Franklin, 1850 [reprint ed. 1970]), xv.

28 Alcaraz, *The Other Side*, 2-3.

29 Griswold del Castillo, *The Treaty*, 115.

30 Alcaraz, *The Other Side*, 450.

31 William A. DePalo, Jr., *The Mexican National Army, 1822-1852* (College Station, Tex.: Texas A&M University Press, 1997), 145-146; and Robert Ryal Miller, *Shamrock and Sword: The Saint Patrick's Battalion in the U.S.-Mexican War* (Norman, Okla.: University of Oklahoma Press, 1989), 135-136.

32 *El Cangrejo* (Mexico City), March 11, 1848; and *El Espíritu del Siglo* (Mexico City), May 25, 1848.

33 DePalo, *The Mexican National Army*.

34 Michael P. Costeloe, "The Mexican Church and the Rebellion of the Polkos," *Hispanic American Historical Review* 46:2 (May 1966), 170-178; and Barbara Tenembaum, "Neither a Borrower nor a Lender Be: Financial Constraints and the Treaty of Guadalupe Hidalgo," in *The Mexican and Mexican American Experience in the Nineteenth Century*, Jaime E. Rodríguez O., ed. (Tempe, Ariz.: Bilingual Press, 1989), 80, 114, n. 43.

35 Pedro Santoni, "The Failure of Mobilization: The Civic Militia of Mexico in 1846," *Mexican Studies/Estudios Mexicanos* 12:2 (Summer 1996), 170-171. The quote is from Timothy Anna, *Forging Mexico, 1821-1835* (Lincoln, Nebr.: University of Nebraska Press 1998), 15.

36 Josefina Zoraida Vázquez, "México y la Guerra con Estados Unidos," in *México al tiempo de su guerra con los Estados Unidos (1846-1848)*, Josefina Zoraida Vázquez, ed. (Mexico City: Fondo de Cultura Económica, 1997), 46.

37 Santoni, "The Failure of Mobilization," 183-184.

38 Lorenzo de Arellano to the minister of Foreign Relations, Guanajuato, July 15, 1847, Benson Latin American Collection, University of Texas at Austin, Justin Smith Papers G 220, xvii, quoted in José Antonio Serrano Ortega, "Hacienda y Guerra, Elites Políticas y Gobierno Nacional. Guanajuato, 1835-1847," in Vázquez, *México al tiempo*, 260-261.

39 Ramírez, *Mexico during the War*, 135.

40 Wellington's quote appears in Allan Peskin, *Winfield Scott and the Profession of Arms* (Kent, Ohio: The Kent State University Press, 2003), 175.

41 Timothy D. Johnson, *Winfield Scott: The Quest for Military Glory* (Lawrence, Kans.: University Press of Kansas, 1998).

42 Timothy Anna, review of Pedro Santoni's *Mexican at Arms: Puro Federalists and the Politics of War, 1845-1848* (Fort Worth, Tex.: Texas Christian University Press, 1996), in *The American Historical Review* 103:2 (April 1998), 627-628.

43 The conspiracy died out by late May 1846. The plotters' maneuvers fueled an extensive domestic opposition movement that equated monarchism with European despotism and depicted it as a threat to Mexico's independence. In addition, by that time the survival of Paredes' government, and thus that of the monarchist plot, came to depend on the success of Mexico's armies over the American forces, but the defeats suffered by Mexican troops early that May at the battles of Palo Alto and Resaca de la Palma sealed the project's fate. See Miguel Soto, *La conspiración monárquica en México, 1845-1846* (Mexico City: EOSA, 1988), and Jaime Delgado, *La monarquía en México, 1845-1847* (Mexico City: Editorial Porrúa, 1990).

44 On this topic, see Santoni, *Mexicans at Arms*, as well as the essays in the volumes edited by Vázquez and Herrera Serna that reveal how individual states and their political leaders reacted to the war.

45 Ramírez, *Mexico During the War*, 152; María del Carmen Vázquez Mantecón, "Santa Anna y su guerra con los angloamericanos: Las versiones de una larga polémica," *Estudios de Historia Moderna y Contemporánea de México* 22 (July-December 2001), 44-45.

46 Zermeño's book was published in Mexico City in 2000 by Nueva Imagen, while Scheina's appeared two years later under the sponsorship of the Washington, DC, publishing house of Brassey's.

47 Enrique Krauze, *Mexico, Biography of Power: A History of Modern Mexico 1810-1996* (New York: Harper Collins, 1997), 151.

48 Fowler, *Mexico in the Age of Proposals*, 5; the quote is in 238.

49 Will Fowler, *Tornel and Santa Anna: The Writer and the Caudillo, Mexico 1795-1853* (Westport, Conn.: Greenwood Press, 2000).

50 Will Fowler, review of DePalo, *The Mexican National Army*, in the *Journal of Latin American Studies* 30:1 (February 1998), 193.

51 DePalo, *The Mexican National Army*, 113-114, 121, and 124. The book does not appraise Santa Anna's orders concerning the evacuation of Tampico.

52 Scheina, *Santa Anna*, 66, 74.

53 Richard Bruce Winders, *Crisis in the Southwest: The United States, Mexico, and the Struggle over Texas* (Wilmington, Del.: Scholarly Resources, 2002), 71-73.

54 Randy Roberts and James S. Olson, *A Line in the Sand: The Alamo in Blood and Memory* (New York: The Free Press, 2001), 55-56.

55 James E. Crisp, *Sleuthing the Alamo: Davy Crockett's Last Stand and Other Mysteries of the Texas Revolution* (New York: Oxford University Press, 2005), 41-42. For a recent assessment of the complex process of shaping the national identities in Mexico's far north, see Andrés Reséndez, *Changing National Identities at the Frontier: Texas and New Mexico, 1800-1850* (New York: Cambridge University Press, 2005).

56 Alcaraz, *The Other Side*, 32.

57 Some historians believe that Polk deliberately sent Slidell to Mexico with erroneous credentials (as minister plenipotentiary rather than as commissioner), while others think that Polk made an honest mistake but found it embarrassing to back down once he became aware of his error. For a representative sample of

where historians stand on this matter, see Piero Gleijeses, "A Brush with Mexico," *Diplomatic History* 29:2 (April 2005), 246, n. 65. A detailed examination of the Slidell mission can be found in David Pletcher, *The Diplomacy of Annexation: Texas, Oregon, and the Mexican War* (Columbia, Mo.: University of Missouri Press, 1973), 286-291, 352-357, 364-374.

58 Gleijeses, "A Brush with Mexico," 223-254. The quoted phrases appear in 223, 234, 243, and 254.

59 Alcaraz, *The Other Side*, 439-442. For Bustamante's remarks, see *El nuevo Bernal*, 1: 18, and 2:176; for Ramírez' perceptions, see *Mexico During the War*, 125-126.

60 Günter Kahle, *El ejército y la formación del Estado en los comienzos de la independencia de México*, María Martínez Peñaloza, trans. (Mexico City: Fondo de Cultura Económica, 1997 [reprint ed. 1969]), 141-145.

61 Irving W. Levinson, *Wars within War: Mexican Guerrillas, Domestic Elites, and the United States of America, 1846-1848* (Fort Worth, Tex. : Texas Christian University Press, 2005), 112-114. The quotes in this paragraph can be found in 113 and 114.

62 Luis Fernando Granados, *Sueñan las piedras: Alzamiento ocurrido en la ciudad de México, 14, 15, y 16 de septiembre de 1847* (Mexico City: Ediciones Era, 2003). For a biographical sketch of Próspero Pérez, see Luis Fernando Granados, "Pequeños patricios, hermanos mayores. Francisco Próspero Pérez como emblema de los sans-culottes capitalinos hacia 1846-1847," *Historias* 54 (January-March 2003), 25-38.

63 William H. Beezley and Linda A. Curcio-Nagy, "Introduction," in *Latin American Popular Culture: An Introduction*, William H. Beezley and Linda A. Curcio-Nagy, eds. (Wilmington, Del.: Scholarly Resources, 2000), xix.

64 The literature on this topic is steadily growing. For a recent example of this type of work see *¡Viva Mexico! ¡Viva La Independencia! Celebrations of September 16*, William H. Beezley and David Lorey, eds. (Wilmington, Del.: Scholarly Resources, 2001).

65 For an in-depth study of how Santa Anna used cultural activities for political purposes, see Shannon Baker Tuller, "Santa Anna's Legacy: Caudillismo in Early Republican Mexico," unpublished. Ph.D. diss., Texas Christian University, 1999. She analyzes the funeral for his leg in 133-138.

66 Enrique Plasencia de la Parra, "Conmemoración de la hazaña épica de los Niños Héroes: Su origen, desarrollo y simbolismos," *Historia Mexicana* 45:2 (October-December 1995), 242-243, 247-248. Also see Vicente Quirarte, "Tiempo de canallas, héroes y artistas. El imaginario de la guerra entre México y Estados Unidos," in *México en guerra*, 71-74.

67 Pedro Santoni, "Where Did the Other Heroes Go? Exalting the '*Polko*' National Guard Battalions in Nineteenth-Century Mexico," *Journal of Latin American Studies* 34 (November 2002): 807-844.

68 Pedro Santoni, "Lucas Balderas: Popular Leader and Patriot," in *The Human Tradition in Mexico*, Jeffrey M. Pilcher, ed. (Wilmington, Del.: Scholarly Resources, 2003), 42, 50-51. The quote is in María Elena Salas Cuesta, coord.

Molino del Rey: historia de un monumento (Mexico City: Consejo Nacional para la Cultura y las Artes, 1997), 226.

69 Santoni, "Lucas Balderas," 52-54.

70 http://gaceta.diputados.gob.mx/Gaceta/Iniciativas/octu1.html.

71 Mónica Matos-Vega, "El recinto de Chapultepec exhibe un discurso de conceptos y temas," in *La Jornada* (Mexico City), Aug. 11, 2005, located in http://www.jornada.unam.mx/ The article does not make clear whether museum officials also gave a new home to the Gabriel Flores mural that depicts Juan Escutia's heroic act. The essay merely states that the wall painting can be viewed on the ceiling of one of the museum's staircases.

72 Mónica Matos-Vega, "Ni tan niños, ni tan héroes," in *La Jornada* (Mexico City), Aug. 11, 2005, located in http://www.jornada.unam.mx/. An earlier attempt to minimize the role of the *Niños Héroes* had ended in abject failure. In 1992 then Minister of Education Ernesto Zedillo authorized the revision of history textbooks for the nation's elementary schools. The new books challenged official mythology by questioning, among other things, the authenticity of the legend of the *Niños Héroes*. The effort did not succeed, as protests by the army, politicians, and teachers led to the recall of nearly seven million volumes. Plasencia de la Parra, "Conmemoración de la hazaña épica," 273-274; and Thomas Benjamin, *La Revolución: Mexico's Great Revolution as Memory, Myth, and History* (Austin: University of Texas Press, 2000), 155.

73 K. Jack Bauer, *The Mexican War, 1846-1848* (Lincoln, Nebr.: University of Nebraska Press, 1992 [reprint. ed. 1974]), 268; and Krystina M. Libura, Luis Gerardo Morales Moreno, and Jesús Velasco Márquez, *Echoes of the Mexican-American War*, Mark Fried, trans. (Toronto: Groundwood Books, 2004), 117.

74 Mónica Matos-Vega, "La codiciada bandera de El Alamo," in *La Jornada* (Mexico City), Aug. 11, 2005, located in http://www.jornada.unam.mx/.

The *Other* War That Remade America
By Elliott West

1 Eighth Census, *Agriculture*, XX; Ninth Census, III, *Industry and Wealth*, 230-31; Tenth Census, III, *Agriculture*, 130.

2 Clark C. Spence, "Western Mining," in Michael P. Malone, ed., *Historians and the American West* (Lincoln: University of Nebraska Press, 1983), 107.

3 The standard work on desire for Pacific ports and farmlands and the role of that desire in our confrontation with Mexico remains Norman A. Graebner, *Empire on the Pacific: A Study in American Continental Expansion* (New York: The Ronald Press Company, 1955).

4 Graebner, *Empire on the Pacific*, 61, 88.

5 William M. Meigs, *Life of Thomas Hart Benton* (Philadelphia, 1904), 308-310; Newman is quoted in W. H. Hickman, "The Coeducation of Races," in

Mohonk Conference on the Negro Question. Reported and Edited by Isabel G. Barrows (1890; reprint, New York: Negro University Press, 1969), 63.

6 For an old standard and new look at the telegraph and its spread, see Alvin F. Harlow, *Old Wires and New Waves: The History of the Telegraph, Telephone, and Wireless* (New York, London: D. Appleton-Century Co., 1936) and Tom Standage, *The Victorian Internet: The Remarkable Story of the Telegraph and the Nineteenth Century's On-Line Pioneers* (New York: Walker and Company, 1998).

7 Oliver Wendell Holmes, "Bread and the Newspaper," *Atlantic Monthly,* 8:45 (July 1861): 348.

8 For an extended look on this law, its origins and history, see John D. Leshy, *The Mining Law: A Study in Perpetual Motion* (Washington, D.C.: Resources for the Future, Inc., 1987).

9 Among the few histories of race in America that consider the term's expanded meaning, see Scott L. Malcomson, *One Drop of Blood: The American Misadventure of Race* (New York: Farrar, Straus and Giroux, 2000).

10 On California of the gold rush as an ethnic stewpot, see Rodman Wilson Paul and Elliott West, *Mining Frontiers of the Far West* (Albuquerque: University of New Mexico Press, 2001), chapter 11.

11 For a more developed discussion on this point, see Elliott West, "Reconstructing Race," *Western Historical Quarterly,* 34:1 (2003): 7-26.

12 Dale E. Watts tallies fifty-six persons killed in politically motivated violence in "Bleeding Kansas." "How Bloody was Bleeding Kansas?: Political Killings in Kansas Territory, 1854-1861," *Kansas History,* 18 (Summer 1995): 116-29.

13 Alan Trachtenberg, *Shades of Hiawatha: Staging Indians, Making Americans, 1880-1930* (New York: Hill and Wang, 2004), 9.

Index